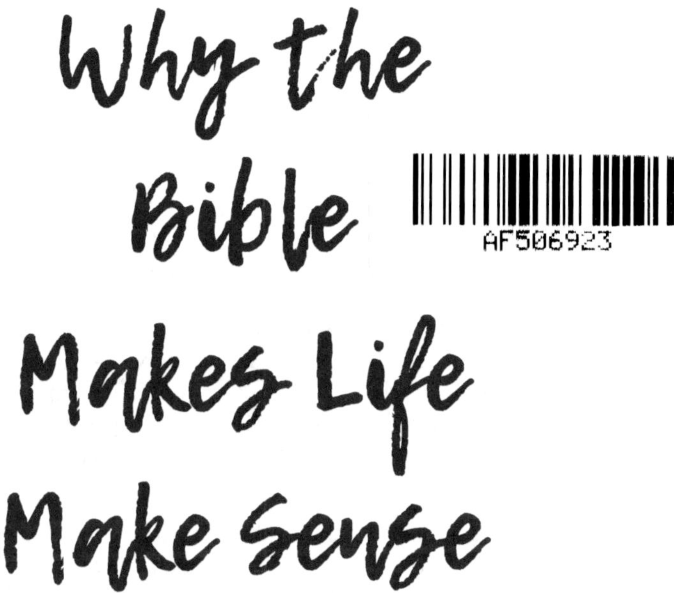

Pursuing a Purposeful Life
from a Biblical Perspective

Heather Erdmann

Table of Contents

Introduction

What would you say is the most pressing question on your mind right now? Is it something to do with your current circumstances? Is it relatively trivial or more profound? Have you ever asked yourself why you're here or pondered your purpose? Does this life have any meaning, or are we all just randomly evolved clumps of cells trying to make sense of an existence without any intrinsic meaning?

Surprisingly, the top 100 questions searched for online in 2024 don't even address these issues. People are more concerned about when the next full moon will occur, how to make money online, and what gluten is.[1] We tend to have a temporal, live-for-the-moment focus on life, while the days and years pass us by and we spend our energy and attention navigating through things that won't matter in a few years, months, or even days. Are we just "going through the motions," or are we living in light of all that life was meant to be?

---

[1] Brian Dean, "100 Most Asked Questions on google in 2024," Exploding Topics, July 18, 2024, https://explodingtopics.com/blog/top-google-questions.

This book was created to help you gain a new perspective and find true purpose and meaning in every area of your life—but it almost wasn't written. As I opened my morning devotional on the second day of a writer's retreat, a Bible verse from the book of Ecclesiastes stopped me before I penned the first words:

Then I saw all the work of God, that man cannot find out the work that is done under the sun. However much man may toil in seeking, he will not find it out. Even though a wise man claims to know, he cannot find it out. (Ecclesiastes 8:17, ESV)

It made me think that maybe I was fooling myself even trying to explain or make sense of this world by taking on a project like this.

So, I prayed again for wisdom and dug deeper into Scripture for meaning and understanding. The book of Ecclesiastes, written by King Solomon, has a spirit of hopeless despair as it explores the futility of life lived "under the sun." He concludes, *"Vanity of vanities, says the Preacher, vanity of vanities! All is vanity. What does man gain by all the toil at which he toils under the sun?" (Ecclesiastes 1:2-3, ESV)*

Yet King Solomon, who had riches and wisdom beyond measure and every form of pleasure available in this world, was showing us that this life and all it encompasses truly would be futile "under the sun" without the eternal perspective that the Bible gives us—

the perspective that provides us with meaning and purpose and that makes this life make sense. We've all heard of celebrities who had everything the world could offer and yet still destroyed themselves with drugs, alcohol, or even suicide as they realized a life lived for temporal pleasures and treasures is not a fulfilling life after all.

The lens through which we view the world shapes how we interpret all areas of life. It's all about perspective. Look at this example when the apostle Paul was shipwrecked on the island of Malta:

When they had been brought safely through, then we found out that the island was called Malta. The natives showed us extraordinary kindness; for because of the rain that had set in and because of the cold, they kindled a fire and received us all. But when Paul had gathered a bundle of sticks and laid them on the fire, a viper came out because of the heat and fastened itself on his hand. When the natives saw the creature hanging from his hand, they began saying to one another, "Undoubtedly this man is a murderer, and though he has been saved from the sea, justice has not allowed him to live." However he shook the creature off into the fire and suffered no harm. But they were expecting that he was about to swell up or suddenly fall down dead. But after they had waited a long time and had seen nothing unusual happen to him, they changed their minds and began to say that he was a god. (Acts 28:1-6)

When the snake bit Paul, the natives, influenced by Greco-Roman lore, concluded he must be a murderer and would surely soon die. Then, when he survived, they changed their assessment of the situation and decided he must be a god! In just a moment, their perspective allowed them to see Paul first as a murderer, and then conversely, as a god. The lens through which they viewed the situation made all the difference in how they interpreted their circumstances.

If we don't have a firm foundation for interpretation, it's like building on shifting sands, and we are at the whim of anything we've ever heard, seen, or thought. Our perspective then becomes an unreliable source of determining the meaning of anything we experience. Everyone has a worldview, and that view shapes how we see every area of our lives, what we value, how we make decisions, and how we determine reality. It's the lens from which we see the world.

Someone once asked me whether delving deeper into the Bible and learning about Christianity strengthened my faith or raised more doubts. I can honestly say that after over 30 years of studying and reading the Bible cover-to-cover multiple times, doubts have been overcome with truth as I see how its principles make sense of every aspect of life, and how God has designed them for our good and His glory. This has only strengthened my faith immeasurably. The Bible is the only book that makes sense of our reality and answers all of life's big questions, giving purpose and meaning to our existence.

It explains such issues as:

- Why are we here?
- What is the meaning of life?
- Where are we going (and how do we get there)?
- How should we live while we are here?
- Why do bad things happen?
- Why is there death?
- How does this all turn out in the end?

And so much more! No other worldview has all the answers the way the Bible does. Through God's own words, He has given us all we need for this life and the next:

For His divine power has granted to us everything pertaining to life and godliness, through the true knowledge of Him who called us by His own glory and excellence. (2 Peter 1:3)

That their hearts may be encouraged, having been knit together in love, and that they would attain to all the wealth that comes from the full assurance of understanding, resulting in a true knowledge of God's mystery, that is, Christ Himself, in whom are hidden all the treasures of wisdom and knowledge. (Colossians 2:2-3)

The *Westminster Confession of Faith* agrees and describes it this way:

The whole counsel of God, concerning all things necessary for His own glory, man's salvation, faith, and life, is either expressly set down in Scripture, or by good and necessary consequence may be deduced from Scripture: unto which nothing at any time is to be added, whether by new revelations of the Spirit, or traditions of men.[2]

Indeed, no human can fully know the mind and ways of God, as He tells us, in Isaiah 55:8-9:

"For My thoughts are not your thoughts, nor are your ways My ways," declares the Lord. "For as the heavens are higher than the earth, so are My ways higher than your ways and My thoughts than your thoughts."

The apostle Paul tells us not to trust the wisdom of the world, but rather to keep looking up with an eye on eternity when he says:

"See to it that no one takes you captive through philosophy and empty deception, according to the tradition of men, according to the elementary principles of the world, rather than according to Christ." (Colossians 2:8)

Knowing Jesus Christ and the God of the Bible gives me a reason to get up each day and to live, love, give, and forgive. That is my hope for you as you read this book. I

____

[2] Scott Oliphint, "Through the Westminster Confession," January 17, 2013, https://www.reformation21.org/confession/2013/01/chapter-16.php.

pray it gives you an eternal perspective that brings purpose and value to your everyday life and makes meaning of the mundane. Throughout this book, you will see how God's Word can bless you with unwavering peace, joy, and hope that can only be found when we know the Author of life and His message to us.

We will start by exploring why the Bible is an extraordinary book, unlike any other because it is the only one where you can commune with the Author every time you read it.

You will also see:

- that it is alive and active with the power to transform hearts, minds, and lives.
- how it spans all of time, yet its principles are timeless.
- how it expresses the full range of human behavior and the complete span of human emotion.
- how it contains one cohesive storyline, though written by more than 40 authors over a span of approximately 1500 years
- and many more features that illustrate how the Bible is truly a supernatural book!

In the second section, we will see how the Bible answers life's most pressing questions and gives us our true purpose and meaning.

Finally, in section three, we will cover the main areas of everyday life that the Bible addresses, including family, marriage, fellowship, education, work, rest, emotions, justice, and morality.

Throughout time, man has attempted to find the meaning of his existence, and throughout this book, you will see how the Bible provides the perspective that truly makes life make sense:

All Scripture is inspired by God and profitable for teaching, for reproof, for correction, for training in righteousness; so that the man of God may be adequate, equipped for every good work. (2 Timothy 3:16-17)

Section One

What's So Special About the Bible?

Chapter 1: The Word is Alive

For the word of God is living and active and sharper than any two-edged sword, and piercing as far as the division of soul and spirit, of both joints and marrow, and able to judge the thoughts and intentions of the heart. (Hebrews 4:12)

It's been said that we can read many books, but the Bible is the only book that reads you. Maybe you've heard a sermon or Biblical message that speaks directly to your current situation or struggle. It's as if the message was directed right at your heart, or as if the preacher had a secret glimpse into your life. Yet it isn't necessarily some special knowledge held by the one delivering the message. Rather, it is the sharpness and precision of the Word of God itself. The Bible is not just an ancient collection of stories or fables. It has inherent life and power. The preacher doesn't make the Word come alive—it IS alive! It is "living" and "active" because it is the mind of the living God in written form.

The Bible is alive because it is "God-breathed" (see 2 Timothy 3:16). The Greek word for this is *theopneustos* with *theo* meaning God, and *pneustos* meaning breathed. It is the only time this word is used in any Greek text including the New Testament.

In John 1:1, we are told:

"In the beginning was the Word, and the Word was with God, and the Word was God."

John also tells us that Jesus, Himself, is the Word made flesh:

And the Word became flesh, and dwelt among us, and we saw His glory, glory as of the only begotten from the Father, full of grace and truth. (John 1:14)

As the living, breathing Son of God, Jesus came to earth to show us the Father and give us the Word of God personified. He taught us who He is and what He is like. Because the Word and God the Father are so intricately related as Jesus proclaimed, *"I and the Father are one"* (John 10:30), the Bible has a power unknown to any other book on earth. It can save and sanctify, inform, and transform. It is by this living and active Word that Jesus created and upholds all things as seen here:

And He is the radiance of His glory and the exact representation of His nature, and upholds all things by the word of His power. When He had made purification of sins, He sat down at the right hand of the Majesty on high. (Hebrews 1:3)

The Bible is effective and impactful because it is empowered by the omnipotent (all-powerful) living God

Himself. We can trust it with our whole hearts, minds, and souls, as we trust the God who wrote it.

The Bible is the written Word of God, and Jesus is the living Word of God. Both reveal God to us and show us who He is and what He is like.[3]

In *The Knowledge of the Holy*, A.W. Tozer writes "A right conception of God is basic not only to systematic theology but to practical Christian living as well." He also stated, "I believe there is scarcely an error in doctrine or a failure in applying Christian ethics that cannot be traced finally to imperfect and ignoble thoughts about God."

You may think that theology, or the study of God, is boring or that it is a topic too high and lofty for you and should be reserved for professors or seminarians. Yet, everyone is a theologian to some degree because everyone has thoughts about God—even atheists who believe He doesn't exist. However, to make sense of this life, we need to know God for who He is rather than who we imagine Him to be. This can only be done through knowledge of His Word.

As we will explore in further detail in a future chapter, God created us to worship. However, who or what we worship depends on where we focus our hearts and

---

[3] Wayne Davies, *Jesus: Who He Is, What He Did and Why It Matters: A Bible Study for Believers and Skeptics, Part 1* (Fort Wayne, IN: Good Messengers Ministries of Fort Wayne, 2015), 27

minds. If we are primarily concerned about ourselves and fulfilling our wants and desires (the default human position), we may end up creating a "god" we can live with—but that only exists in our minds.

A traditional quote says, "Men do not reject the Bible because it contradicts itself, but because it contradicts them."[4]

If we find ourselves saying, "To me, God is…" we may be guilty of idolatry or trying to conform God to our likeness rather than getting to know Him as He truly is and how He has revealed Himself to us in His Word. He wants us to know Him personally, going so far as to send us His only begotten Son, our Lord Jesus, to come to earth and live among us in the flesh. The Bible is filled with eyewitness accounts of those who interacted with Jesus while He lived on earth, observed His miracles, and heard His teachings. We get to know Him as we read those accounts in the pages of Scripture.

We Can Interact with the Author

Because the Bible is a living book, it is also the only one in which you can interact with the Author every time you read it. As you do, you can pause to pray, offer thanksgiving, ask questions, confess sins, or claim His promises as they apply. We don't just read the Bible to gain information, although we do that as well. But,

---

4 "Bible," Sermon Illustrations, accessed April 27, 2024, https://www.sermonillustrations.com/a-z/b/bible.htm.

more importantly, He "meets us" in His Word as the Holy Spirit works through it and in and through us. As believers, we have the privilege of having the Author of Scripture, the Holy Spirit, living inside us to help us understand and apply it as seen here:

"But the Helper, the Holy Spirit, whom the Father will send in My name, He will teach you all things, and bring to your remembrance all that I said to you." (John 14:26)

The Bible also tells us that without His help, its truths are not fully knowable to those who read it without faith. Unbelievers, who do not have the Holy Spirit, cannot fully grasp the depths of truth that the Scriptures reveal:

But a natural man does not accept the things of the Spirit of God, for they are foolishness to him; and he cannot understand them, because they are spiritually appraised. (1 Corinthians 2:14)

Jesus is not only the "Word made flesh", but also "the way, the truth, and the life," (from John 1:14 and 14:6). He is the only way to the Father in heaven and our only hope for eternal life because He is the only one who has dealt with our sin problem. The Bible is the source of the Gospel message which points us to Jesus, the only one with the power to save our souls and bring dead sinners to life.

Here are some examples where Scripture clearly shows us this:

"Truly, truly, I say to you, he who hears My word, and believes Him who sent Me, has eternal life, and does not come into judgment, but has passed out of death into life." (John 5:24)

Receive the word implanted, which is able to save your souls. (James 1:21b)

For I am not ashamed of the gospel, for it is the power of God for salvation to everyone who believes, to the Jew first and also to the Greek. (Romans 1:16)

For you have been born again not of seed which is perishable but imperishable, that is, through the living and enduring word of God. (1 Peter 1:23)

Like a seed, the Gospel message brings forth life as it is planted in our hearts and minds. In the "Parable of the Sower" in Matthew 13:1-23, Jesus tells us that God's Word is like a seed and that how it grows and bears fruit depends on the type of soil onto which it falls. Seed sown on rocky soil is received with joy, but it has no root and falls away when trouble and persecution come because of the Word. Seed sown on thorns gets choked out by worries and wealth and produces no fruit. But, when planted on good soil, the seed can flourish and bear much fruit. We are the soil, and the power of the Word works in us according to our receptiveness to it.

It is Food for Our Souls

The Bible is not only profitable for our salvation, but it is food for our souls. It helps strengthen, equip, deliver, and transform us. When Jesus was here on earth, He proclaimed that the Word of God is even more important than our daily food:

But He answered, "It is written, "'Man shall not live by bread alone, but by every word that comes from the mouth of God.'" (Matthew 4:4, ESV)

The Bible is filled with prayers, poems, songs, and stories that can strengthen us when we feel weak or weary. It helps deliver us from temptation as we run to God in His Word and transforms our lives as we live by its truths. It equips us for the daily battles we face in this life and gives us the armor of God to protect our hearts, minds, and souls (see Ephesians 6:10-20).

It is A Weapon for Battle

Ephesians 6:17 tells us that God's Word, referred to as "the sword of the Spirit," is given to us to accomplish victory in the spiritual battles we face. It has inherent power, and when we wield it correctly, we have access to that power!

Jesus also used the Scriptures in His fight against temptation from the devil in the wilderness when He quoted the Old Testament and affirmed the authority of God's Word (see Matthew 4:1-11 and Luke 4:1-13).

The Bible can not only be used as an offensive weapon in our arsenal, but as a defensive weapon with the ability to heal and deliver us from oppression, strongholds, and all manner of destruction as we see here:

He sent His word and healed them, and delivered them from their destructions. (Psalm 107:20)

When evening came, they brought to Him many who were demon-possessed; and He cast out the spirits with a word, and healed all who were ill. (Matthew 8:16)

Jesus cast out demons by the power of His Word, and God delivers us from the devil and our sinful flesh as His Word convicts us of sin. As noted earlier, a preacher's message can often "cut to the heart." Have you ever heard a passage or verse that makes you say, "Ouch!"? That's because the Bible is sharper than a two-edged sword (see Hebrews 4:12), and it can discern our motives, thoughts, and intentions. It lays bare our hearts and exposes them in truth.

Jesus confirmed that the Holy Spirit would come and convict us in John 16:8 when He said, *"And He, when He comes, will convict the world concerning sin and righteousness and judgment."*

As the Holy Spirit works through His Word, we see where we fall short of God's standards. This leads us to the cross of Christ to find forgiveness in Him. The Word is like a mirror that shows us our true heart condition and points us to Jesus, the only One who can help us.

It Accomplishes God's Purposes

Not only does the Bible work on us and in us, but God also uses it to accomplish His work in the world through us. The prophet Isaiah tells us that the Bible is effectual and that God uses it to accomplish all things according to His will:

So will My word be which goes out of My mouth; It will not return to Me empty, without accomplishing what I desire, and without succeeding in the purpose for which I sent it. (Isaiah 55:11)

What other book or author can make that kind of claim?

God uses His Word to accomplish His will, and one of His main objectives is to conform us to the image of Christ and make us more like Jesus through a process called "sanctification". The dictionary defines sanctification as making or declaring something holy or morally acceptable, and the Bible accomplishes this by renewing and transforming us through its principles and truths. Jesus confirmed it when He said:

"Sanctify them in the truth; Your word is truth." (John 17:17)

It is Our Source of Truth

As the living Word, Jesus Himself is "the Truth" (see John 14:6). That is why the Bible should be our ultimate source of reality in every aspect of our lives. This foundation of truth liberates us and sets us free to live the fullest, most purposeful lives that God intended according to His ways.

One problem with the world today is that there is a war on truth. People claim exclusive rights to define it however they decide under the guise of "living out their truth." Yet this problem isn't new. The battle has always been for what is right and true. The devil's first lie questioned God's Word when he asked, *"Did God really say?"* (see Genesis 3:1).

But Jesus told us, *"And you will know the truth, and the truth will make you free"* (see John 8:32). This refers to the saving truth of the Gospel—not "my truth" or "your truth" but *the* Truth!

Throughout time, people have wrestled with and twisted the Scriptures to say whatever they wanted them to mean. However, truth is not relative. Truth is a Person, and His name is Jesus.

Fulfilled Prophecies

The Bible proves itself true when we consider the numerous fulfilled prophecies and predictions made about the person and work of Jesus Christ, hundreds and thousands of years before He came in the flesh.

Prophets made both general and specific claims about the identity and ministry of the promised Messiah, and Jesus fulfilled them all!

Conservative estimates tell us that He fulfilled at least 300 prophecies regarding His first coming.[5] The number is even higher when considering indirect references and allusions to Christ in the Old Testament. The mathematical probability of one man doing this is beyond human comprehension! If He had fulfilled only eight of the over 300 prophecies, the chance of doing so would be 10^{17}—a 10 with seventeen zeroes behind it! Forty-eight fulfilled prophecies would give us 10^{157}! Anyone can make predictions, but having them come true, especially hundreds or thousands of years after they were made, is something supernatural! It attests to the fact that the Bible truly is a divine book and the source of all truth.

It is the only book ever written that is completely God-breathed, living, personal, transformative, protective, sanctifying, and comforting. It provides food for our souls in this life and points us to the Lord Jesus Christ who has the power to save and give us eternal life. Our unchanging God is the Author, and because of that, we can trust it to make this life make sense!

---

[5] "How Many Prophecies Did Jesus Fulfill?" GotQuestions.org, accessed August 12, 2023, https://www.gotquestions.org/prophecies-of-Jesus.html.

Chapter 2: One Cohesive Storyline

Then beginning with Moses and with all the prophets, He explained to them the things concerning Himself in all the Scriptures. (Luke 24:27)

What if you could find one book that was an action, adventure, history, mystery, and romance in one? What if it also contained wisdom, poetry, and prophecy? This book has been written, and all of these are contained in the pages of Scripture. The Holy Bible is the greatest-selling book of all time with over five billion copies sold,[6] and for good reason.

It is divinely inspired, which makes it amazing for that fact alone. However, several other features make it a unique, one-of-a-kind book. Written over a period spanning at least 1500 years, the one book we call the Bible consists of 66 smaller books written by around 40 different human authors from various occupations. Considering the duration over which it was penned and

---

6 Mark Manson, "The 24 Best Selling Books of All Time," accessed September 8, 2023, https://markmanson.net/best-books/best-selling-books-all-time.

the sheer multitude of writers, it is truly a miracle that this collection of ancient writings tells one cohesive story. God's plan of redemption for a fallen world, through His Son, our Lord Jesus Christ, is what the Bible is truly all about.

This description from the apologetics organization Stand to Reason expands on the details and explains it well:

The Bible consists of sixty-six books written by forty or more authors from diverse backgrounds (rabbis, warriors, shepherds, kings, historians), in a diversity of conditions (dungeons, deserts, battlefields, palaces, pastures), on a diversity of controversial subjects, over a fifteen-hundred-year period of time.

The Bible doesn't read like sixty-six different stories, though. Instead, a profound harmony of perspective is woven through the account from Genesis to Revelation as God progressively unveils his rescue plan for fallen creation.

No individual writer understood the plan completely. Each in his time, as if guided by an unseen hand, added his piece to the puzzle. Later, at the advent of Christ, all the pieces come together, revealing the full picture of God's strategy for salvation that had been unfolding for ages.

This remarkable continuity defies naturalistic explanation.[7]

It was never meant to be read in bits and pieces or reduced to isolated events and moral imperatives. It is not primarily a "rule book for life"—although it serves that purpose as well. It is a book that highlights God and points us to Him and His character and plan. When we keep this big-picture narrative in mind, with Jesus as the hero of the story and we as the beneficiaries of God's plan of redemption through Him, the whole book takes on a new perspective. This helps us to correctly interpret all the seemingly random bits and pieces, which on their own may or may not make sense or can be taken out of context.

This central storyline of Scripture shows us that God has always planned to save fallen humans through the coming of a rescuer, the promised Messiah, our Lord Jesus Christ. All of it points to this plan of salvation and displays the attributes and glory of God. In the opening scene of Genesis, He created a perfect world and a people to love and with whom He would have a relationship. Then quickly, conflict ensued when those first humans rebelled against their Creator. It was then that sin, suffering, and death entered the story:

When the woman saw that the tree was good for food, and that it was a delight to the eyes, and that the tree

---

[7] Greg Koukl, "Ancient Words, Ever True?," November 1, 2023, https://www.str.org/w/ancient-words-ever-true-.

was desirable to make one wise, she took from its fruit and ate; and she gave also to her husband with her, and he ate. Then the eyes of both of them were opened, and they knew that they were naked; and they sewed fig leaves together and made themselves loin coverings. (Genesis 3:6-7)

Man's stain of sin separated him from a perfect and holy God, and the story seemed to be over without hope as quickly as it began. Thankfully, God revealed His plan shortly after that when He promised to send a divine deliverer who would rescue them:

And I will put enmity between you and the woman, and between your seed and her seed; He shall bruise you on the head, and you shall bruise him on the heel." *(Genesis 3:15)*

From this point forward, God's promise to send a Messiah who would save His people is anticipated throughout the Old Testament. This expectancy drives the narrative as we read Scripture with a Christ-centered lens, looking for the promised One to come. The New Testament Gospels showcase His arrival and life here on earth, with the remaining New Testament books looking back on His first coming and forward to our eternity with Him when He comes again for His bride the church.

Interestingly, this storyline unfolds in many different literary genres throughout the 66 books that comprise the Bible. So, knowing the main message of God's Word helps us make sense of every story, proverb, poem, and prophecy we read.

The Hebrew Bible, or Old Testament, consists primarily of the Law or Torah (the first five books of the Bible), and the Psalms, Proverbs, and Prophets. It was divided into three main sections: the Torah, the Writings, and the Prophets. It was the Old Testament Scriptures that Jesus referred to in Luke 24:27 when He appeared to the men on the road to Emmaus after His resurrection. As He explained the passages to them, He showed how the promises and prophecies all pointed to Him!

In the Gospel of John, Jesus stated it this way:

"You search the Scriptures because you think that in them you have eternal life; it is these that testify about Me." (John 5:39)

Jesus outlined the promises of His coming and specific details of His life throughout the text as He showed them the Old Testament prophecies He had fulfilled. Here is an overview of these prophecies followed by the New Testament verses confirming them:

Genesis 3:15—born of the seed of a woman (Galatians 4:4)

Genesis 12:2-3—born in the line of Abraham (Matthew 1:1)

Genesis 49:10—from the tribe of Judah (Luke 3:33)

Isaiah 7:14—born of a virgin (Luke 1:26-27, 30-31)

Isaiah 9:7—heir to the throne of David (Luke 1:32-33)

Micah 5:2—born in Bethlehem (Luke 2:4-7)

Psalm 2:7—declared the Son of God (Hebrews 1:5)

Psalm 110:4—a priest after the order of Melchizedek (Hebrews 5:5-6)

Zechariah 9:9—triumphal entry on Palm Sunday (John 12:14-16)

Zechariah 11:12-13—sold for thirty pieces of silver (Matthew 26:15, 27:3-10)

Isaiah 53:12—vicarious sacrifice (1 Peter 2:21-25)

Psalm 22:16—hands and feet pierced (Luke 24:39-40)

Psalm 34:20—no bones broken (John 19:34-37)

Psalm 16:10, 49:15—would rise from the dead (Luke 24:6)

This small sample shows the important details predicted about Jesus, hundreds and thousands of years before He came to earth. The entire Bible weaves His story throughout and points to this promised Savior.

Four Main Themes

Throughout these genres, we see four main themes repeated as the story progresses:

1. Creation
2. Fall
3. Redemption
4. Restoration

These themes play out repeatedly throughout the narrative. We already noted three of these themes as Genesis opened with creation, quickly resulted in a fall, and was ultimately given the hope of redemption through a promised Messiah. From Genesis to the final book of Revelation, God used people, places, ideas, and situations to foreshadow this plan of salvation and point to an ultimate victory and restoration when Christ returns to make all things new:

And He who sits on the throne said, "Behold, I am making all things new." And He said, "Write, for these words are faithful and true." (Revelation 21:5)

Types and Shadows of Christ

Ever since I was very young, I've loved books and stories that give hints and glimpses of information about what will be revealed as the story concludes. In fourth grade, I had an amazing teacher who fostered creative writing in many ways and encouraged me to use my God-given gifts as an author. It was then, at nine years old, that I found myself incorporating these foreshadowing techniques into my work wherever possible. That is one of the many reasons I love God's Word so much. He does this throughout the Bible as He points us to Jesus. It has been said that Christ is anticipated in the Old Testament, revealed in the Gospels, proclaimed in the book of Acts, explained in the Epistles, and returns in triumph in the book of Revelation.

These types and shadows that point to Jesus are even more evident as we look at how God chose the nation of Israel as His people through which He would send the promised Messiah and reveal Himself to the world. Other nations would see how God supernaturally blessed, protected, and provided for them as they worshiped Him, and they would know He was the one true God. The Old Testament details the history of the Jewish people through Abraham's descendants. The promises and covenants God made with them ultimately led to His plan of salvation for all of us through Christ. Here we see the promise God made to Abraham:

"Indeed I will greatly bless you, and I will greatly multiply your seed as the stars of the heavens and as the sand which is on the seashore; and your seed shall possess the gate of their enemies. In your seed all the nations of the earth shall be blessed, because you have obeyed My voice." (Genesis 22:17-18)

As we read about Israel, we see repeated patterns of rebellion and disobedience, resulting in cycles of discipline, followed by repentance, forgiveness, and restoration. This foreshadows our own story and shows us how we fit into God's plan. As fallen humans, we are all guilty of sin and have been separated from God. Yet His promises apply not only to Israel but to us, too, when we receive them by faith and also become God's children as seen here:

Know then that it is those of faith who are the sons of Abraham. And the Scripture, foreseeing that God would justify the Gentiles by faith, preached the gospel beforehand to Abraham, saying, "In you shall all the nations be blessed." (Galatians 3:7-8, ESV)

The Old Testament narratives are filled with symbolic references to Jesus. It is important to read the Scriptures with this Christo-centric lens to ascertain the full meaning of the text. For example, the elaborate description of the temple and the Old Testament sacrificial system all pointed to Jesus, the Lamb of God, who was the only fully sufficient sacrifice for our sins. Ultimately, the Old Testament altar points to the New Testament cross.

Keeping in mind that the entire Bible points to Jesus as the hero, it's important that we not insert ourselves into the narrative unless the context permits it. When we read stories of rescuers like David in the story of David and Goliath, we should not be tempted to make ourselves the star by thinking the scene is about us overcoming our troubles (our "Goliaths") if we just bravely persevere. Remembering the Bible is ultimately a book about God, we can then see how it illustrates David, who defeated Goliath and saved Israel, as an example of Jesus who triumphed over our enemies and rescued us when we were powerless to do so ourselves.

At first glance, the sixty-six smaller books that make up the Bible can seem overwhelming or feel somewhat random or disjointed. Yet, when we remember that the Bible is one cohesive story with Jesus as the hero, we see how He is promised, anticipated, proclaimed, and explained throughout its pages. When we keep the four main themes of creation, fall, redemption, and restoration in mind we see these aspects throughout the Bible. We can ask ourselves, "What part of the story is this showing me?" and "How does it point to Jesus?"

The more we read and study God's Word with this Christ-centered view, the more we see the repeated themes, elaborate connections, fascinating patterns, and symbolic images that all serve a purpose to advance the Bible's main message. It's like a treasure hunt and revealed mystery in one! As you seek God expectantly and diligently in His Word, He reveals more and more truth over time. The more He reveals, the more your faith in Him and love for Him will grow as you see just how you fit into His marvelous plan!

Chapter 3: Timeless Truth (for Truthless Times)

Jesus Christ is the same yesterday and today and forever. (Hebrews 13:8)

Whether you've lived 20, 40, 60, 80, or more years here on Earth, you've probably seen numerous changes in your life. Whether it be the prevailing culture, clothing styles, musical genres, family dynamics, or even your own tastes and preferences, life offers many twists and turns—some positive, some negative, and some simply neutral. Thankfully, amidst all the uncertainty that life affords, we have a solid foundation on which to build our lives. We can take comfort in the certainty that is God and His Word.

The Author Transcends Time

Critics may say the Bible is an outdated, ancient manuscript that no longer applies to our modern times. Yet, the Bible is timeless because God is timeless. The same one who inspired the words of Scripture existed before time began, and because He is eternal, He also already exists in the future. It's mind-boggling, but God transcends the time boundaries that constrain us as mortal humans. Although the concept of human time is based on the earthly life of Jesus and is divided into B.C. and A.D. which stand for "Before Christ" and "Anno Domini," which means "in the Year of the Lord," no words can fully describe the timelessness of our infinite God.

When He inspired the authors to pen the Bible's words, He intended them to endure for all time. They would never become obsolete. He was not unaware of future circumstances or current times. Nothing is new or a surprise to God. Those who say that the Bible is outdated or that the original writers of Scripture didn't foresee future cultural or societal changes forget that God is the ultimate Author and that He is outside of time. It is the height of arrogance to say that we, mere creations of His, know more than He did when the Holy Spirit inspired His Word to be written by men of God's own choosing. He is always with us and is never out of touch with our current circumstances. The Bible is still as applicable today as it was originally because its principles are still true and can be applied to all situations and experiences when taken in their respective contexts. It teaches us wisdom, guides our decisions, corrects us when we lose our way, comforts us in times of trouble, and prepares us for this life and the next. The Bible never changes because God never changes as we see here:

"Heaven and earth will pass away, but My words will not pass away." (Matthew 24:35)

"For truly I say to you, until heaven and earth pass away, not the smallest letter or stroke shall pass from the Law until all is accomplished." (Matthew 5:18)

Jesus Christ is the same yesterday and today and forever. (Hebrews 13:8)

God Preserves His Word

Critics also claim that the Bible has been changed throughout the years, like a game of "telephone" where the original texts are somewhere lost in translation. But a God who is powerful enough to create all things is powerful enough to preserve His Word for us as He intended throughout time. To say that man changed it somehow is to say that God is not completely in control, or that He is not the sovereign ruler of all. It supposes that man could thwart God's will. There have been different translations of the Bible into a multitude of languages, and there have been updated versions of those translations to reflect the evolution of vocabulary over the years. Yet by God's providence, the main doctrines and message of the Bible have remained consistent. Numerous historical and archaeological sources have confirmed the accuracy of today's Bible. Although the enormous amounts of proof and research are beyond the scope of this book, we can rest assured that the Bible is historically accurate and verifiable as recorded in numerous texts including ancient literature, government documents, and analyzed archaeological evidence. Modern publications such as the trade journal *Biblical Archaeological Review* verify its historicity time and time again. The Bible contains eyewitness accounts that detail such specifics as weather conditions, names of provincial rulers, and other minute details that verify their accuracy. Even Jesus Himself quoted the Old Testament writings as Scripture and acknowledged them as the words of God:

Now He said to them, "These are My words which I spoke to you while I was still with you, that all things which are written about Me in the Law of Moses and the Prophets and the Psalms must be fulfilled." (Luke 24:44)

In 1947, when the Dead Sea Scrolls were found in a cave in Qumran, near the West Bank of Israel, linguistic experts confirmed that these Old Testament texts, containing parts of every book in the Old Testament except for Esther and dating from as early as the third century B.C., were over 95% word-for-word accurate to the previously known texts from 930 A.D.—with over 1000 years of transmission between them.[8] We can trust our Bible because we can trust our God. His master plan will always prevail!

The Word Became Flesh

Our God is not only sovereign, powerful, and unchanging, He is a personal God. Christianity is the only religion where God Himself stepped into time and

---

[8] Patrick Zukeran, "The Dead Sea Scrolls Shed Light on the Accuracy of our Bible," Probe for Answers, April 17, 2006, https://probe.org/the-dead-sea-scrolls/.

became fully human like us, while also remaining fully divine.

God in the flesh, in the person of Jesus Christ, walked the earth with us in historically verifiable and eyewitness accounts. Because He became one of us, the Bible also provides us with a valuable identity in a world sorely suffering from an identity crisis. When we see that we were made by God and for God, to give Him glory and receive His love and blessings, it gives us purpose and makes our lives make sense. It's not all about us, and that is a freeing reality!

Timeless Truth for Living

With all the current confusion about truth, gender, reality, and morality, the Bible is our unchanging source of timeless truths. Its principles, rightly applied, give us a road map to eternity and applicable wisdom for how to live this life here and now. The book of Proverbs alone has 31 chapters and 915 verses with practical life principles. We can use the Bible to navigate relationships, work, and every aspect of daily life. For example, 1 Thessalonians 5:18 reminds us to always be thankful, 1 Corinthians 6:19-20 tells us to take good care of our bodies to glorify God, and Luke 6:31 gives us "The Golden Rule" to treat others the way we want to be treated.

Past, Present, and Future

Another fascinating aspect of time and timelessness concerning the Bible is that it encompasses events that span all of human time, before time began, and beyond time into eternity. It starts by giving a glimpse of God before He created us, letting us see His eternality as He states, *"I AM WHO I AM"* (see Exodus 3:14), and showing us that God has always existed without beginning or end. Then, it details the beginning of time, the creation of the world, and the history of man with future prophecies of the coming Messiah, which we now know have been fulfilled in Jesus. It continues to detail time through the end of this age and into eternity. Covering the span of human history from before time began and into our eternal future, the Bible is once again an incomparable book. Jesus tells us He is from first to last, and beginning to end in the book of Revelation:

"I am the Alpha and the Omega, the first and the last, the beginning and the end." (Revelation 22:13)

Already-Not Yet

Interestingly, although the Bible's timeline is primarily linear in structure, it also has some remarkable examples of the dual nature of time and truths that cover an "already-not yet" phenomenon. Several of God's promises not only affected the people they were made to but often had future implications as well. For example, David was promised an eternal heir to his kingly throne—a promise made as a future prediction. Yet, it also looked backward to Abraham to whom God promised that the Messiah would come from Abraham's descendants. It ultimately pointed forward to the King who reigns forever, namely our Lord and Savior Jesus! That promise made to David also looked even further ahead to include us, who would live and reign with Jesus forever when we are saved by grace through faith in Him. If we were to place these promises on a timeline, we could see how they are progressive and have applications for both the current recipient as well as future successors:

God's promise to <u>Abraham</u> that the world would be blessed through his future descendant pointed ahead to→ God's promise to <u>David</u> that a King from his line would reign forever, which pointed ahead to→ <u>Jesus</u>, the fulfillment of both those promises and ultimately to→ God's promise of eternal life to <u>us</u> through faith in Jesus who is the descendant of Abraham, the Son of David, and the King who reigns forever!

Another example of the "already-not yet" concept is seen in Luke 17:20-30 where Jesus talked about the Kingdom of God. He referred to the fact that the Kingdom had "already" arrived as He displayed His power over both the physical and spiritual world through miracles and the casting out of demons. He also explained the "not yet" of the complete fulfillment of His Kingdom in the future when He will return to restore all things and triumph over death, sin, and evil forever.

On an even more personal level, as believers, we have the "already" reality of being justified (meaning declared "not guilty"—or "just as if I had never sinned") because we have been forgiven of all our sins through faith in Christ the moment we believe the Gospel. We also have the ongoing reality of our sanctification, which is the process by which He makes us more like Jesus, day by day. Finally, we have the future or "not yet" reality of our glorification which will occur when we leave this earthly life and enter eternity with Him. We can see this time phenomenon explained in Romans which describes the past when God chose us, the present where He calls and justifies us, and the future when He will glorify us in eternity:

And these whom He predestined, He also called; and these whom He called, He also justified; and these whom He justified, He also glorified. (Romans 8:30)

Not only does the Bible cover time and eternity, but it is unique in that it showcases the full span of human behavior and expresses the full spectrum of human emotion as we will see next.

The Full Span of Human Behavior

From the worst of the worst to the ultimate best, we see human behavior on display in all its forms throughout the pages of Scripture. It doesn't take long for the depth of the depravity of man to be seen. By the fourth chapter of Genesis, the first murder occurs:

Cain spoke to Abel his brother. And when they were in the field, Cain rose up against his brother Abel and killed him. (Genesis 4:8, ESV)

The Bible is filled with horrific examples of human pride, jealousy, cruelty, injustice, greed, deception, betrayal, immorality, rape, adultery, murder, and war including:

- In Genesis chapters 37-50, where we see Joseph, the son of Jacob, sold into slavery by his jealous brothers, betrayed by his boss's wife, and thrown into prison unjustly for a crime he didn't commit.
- In Exodus chapters 1-15, we see the enslavement and cruel treatment of the entire nation of Israel in Egypt for over 400 years.
- The book of Judges, chapter 16, tells of a woman named Delilah who tricked her husband, Samson, through deception that led to his capture, enslavement, the gouging out of his eyes, and his eventual death.
- Judges chapter 19 has one of the worst examples of human depravity ever imagined. A Levite and his concubine stayed the night with a man in Gibeah, and men from the town pounded on his door to have sinful relations with the Levite visitor. In a shocking turn of events, the

concubine is sent out to the men who rape and abuse her all night, leaving her for dead on the man's doorstep. Taking her lifeless body home, the Levite man cut her into twelve pieces and sent them to all the tribes of Israel to show the atrocity that occurred. It was a horrific and contemptible act of violence and evil that illustrates the depths of corruption that sinful man is capable of committing.

- The book of Esther records the account of a prideful man named Haman, one of the King of Persia's top officials, who plotted to destroy the entire Jewish people when Mordecai, a Jewish man, refused to bow down to him.

- Even one of the most beloved and well-known people in the Bible, King David, was guilty of adultery and murder as exposed in the book of 2 Samuel.

- In the New Testament, just shortly after Jesus's birth, King Herod the Great of Judea, made a decree to destroy all male infants under the age of two years old in the vicinity of Bethlehem because he feared the promised King of the Jews prophesied to be born during his reign (see Matthew 2:1-16).

- Later, King Herod Antipas's wife, Herodias, ordered the beheading of John the Baptist because she was furious that he had publicly denounced her illegitimate marriage to Herod after divorcing his half-brother (see Matthew 14:1-12, Mark 6:14-29).

- The Gospels tell us of one of Jesus's twelve apostles, Judas Iscariot, who betrayed him for thirty pieces of silver (see Matthew 26:15). This shows that even those closest to us can be capable of unimaginable deception and betrayal.

But the most egregious act of evil human behavior is displayed in the cruel mocking, scourging, and crucifixion of the perfect God-man Jesus Christ recorded in all four Gospels (see Matthew 27, Mark 15, Luke 23, and John 19). Not one ounce of sin or shame was found in Him nor warranted the brutal punishment and death He suffered. Yet He did it as part of God's plan of redemption for all of us.

That horrific event brings us to the glorious other end of the spectrum of human behavior displayed in Scripture. The Bible gives many examples that display considerable love and selflessness as seen here:

- Forgiveness was demonstrated when Joseph forgave his brothers for their evil acts against him in Genesis 50:15-21.
- Moses displayed bravery as he confronted the cruel Egyptian pharaoh and God used him to rescue the Israelites from slavery in the book of Exodus chapters 1-15.
- David exhibited repentance and contrition for sin when confronted about his adultery and murder in 2 Samuel 12.

- Esther, from the book of the same name, was a young Jewish woman who modeled selflessness and courage when she risked her life to approach the Persian king about sparing the lives of her people that the wicked Haman had tried to destroy.
- In the New Testament, many people are familiar with the story of the Good Samaritan who took care of the man who had been beaten, robbed, and left to die on the side of the road. This showcases the depths of human compassion and unconditional love triumphing over the presence of evil and suffering Luke 10:29-37.

Yet, the most compassionate, selfless demonstration of love that ever occurred was when Christ willingly forfeited His life so that we could be forgiven of our sins and saved eternally. No other display of kindness, mercy, and grace compares to what Jesus did for us:

"For God so loved the world, that He gave His only begotten Son, that whoever believes in Him shall not perish, but have eternal life." (John 3:16)

Once again, we see how the Bible is unique as, throughout its pages, the full span of human behavior is on display. This doesn't mean the Bible condones or approves of any of the evil actions that occurred. Rather it records the reality of the nature of a fallen human race and displays the depth of our depravity and our need for a Savior. It also showcases the goodness that comes from hearts fully submitted to Him.

The Full Spectrum of Human Emotion

Scripture is also unique in that it covers the full spectrum of human emotion. No other book in history showcases each possible feeling quite like the Bible. Everything from the depths of despair to the heights of joy can be found. Even God displays His emotions in its pages. A wide range can be seen in just this one verse from the Psalms:

For His anger is but for a moment, His favor is for a lifetime; Weeping may last for the night, but a shout of joy comes in the morning. (Psalm 30:5)

The Psalms are filled with prayers and poetry showcasing the total realm of human sentiment imaginable. They are a great place to go for comfort when experiencing sorrow, encouragement when feeling depressed, or praise and worship during times of rejoicing. The Psalms are filled with laments and longings, hope and happiness, prayers and promises, and even hints of prophecy that all point to the ultimate joy we find in Jesus!

A Book Without Equal

These are just some of the numerous reasons why the Bible is an extraordinary book with no equal. Not only is it a living book, with a divine Author, but it has timeless truths, wisdom for this world, practical applications, purposeful promises, predictive prophecies, and comfort for all conditions. It is our weapon for life's battles, our source of unwavering truth, and food for our souls. It also gives us our identity knowing we are made by God and for God. It gives life meaning and purpose beyond anything this temporal world can offer. Earth and time may pass away, but God's word assures us that it will endure forever:

"Heaven and earth will pass away, but My words will not pass away." (Matthew 24:35)

As David Guzik writes, in the *Enduring Word Commentary*:

- There is no book like it in its continuity and consistency.
- There is no book like it in its honesty.
- There is no book like it in its circulation.
- There is no book like it in its survival.
- There is no book like it in its life-changing power.[9]

Truly the Bible is one of a kind, and it is the only book that makes life make sense!

---

[9] David Guzik, "2 Timothy 3 – Perilous Times and Precious Truth," Enduring Word, 2018, https://enduringword.com/bible-commentary/2-timothy-3/.

The Bible Answers

Life's Big Questions

Chapter 4: The Meaning of Life

Grace and peace be multiplied to you in the knowledge of God and of Jesus our Lord; seeing that His divine power has granted to us everything pertaining to life and godliness, through the true knowledge of Him who called us by His own glory and excellence. (2 Peter 1:2-3)

How Did We Get Here?

In our current, post-Christian world, which is saturated in Darwinian evolution, any other viewpoint of how we came into being is highly controversial. Both creationists and evolutionists have access to the same evidence. What differs is how that evidence is interpreted. Your perspective on this subject will profoundly affect how you view life in general. It will affect your choices, decisions, politics, and how you make sense of the world around you. The magnitude of the debate between evolution and creation is beyond the scope of this book. (For more information on this topic, a great place to start would be *Answers in Genesis* which can be found at **www.answersingenesis.org**.) However, I intend to show you just how a Biblical view of creation gives meaning and purpose to life where no other explanation does.

Although there are other opinions of our origins, for the sake of simplicity and clarity, we will look at the two prevailing positions including creationism where an all-powerful deity created life, and evolution where organisms developed on their own over a span of billions of years. The theory of evolution, however, does not account for how these organisms actually began, and it also conversely acknowledges that scientists observe that new life only comes from existing life. The law that life only comes from life has never been violated under observation or experimentation. Charles Darwin himself also acknowledged that the fossil record would be critical to upholding his theory. Yet after almost 200 years of research, not one credible "missing link" fossil has been found to validate his hypothesis. Although micro-evolution, or adaptation within a species, *is* provable and observable, Darwinian macro-evolution, or adaptation from one lower-level species or kind to another, is still only a "theory." It is a philosophy, and not a scientific, provable fact—although those who deny God or defend the theory hold to it as if their very existence depended on it (pun intended).

Without a creator, they surmise they are not accountable to anyone and can effectively be gods unto themselves. But, if we carry the theory of evolution to its logical conclusion, that we are mere accidents of nature caused by random chance, the implications are dismal and offer no hope for this life or beyond. Without a transcendent, moral God, there can be no objective measure of good or evil, right or wrong. If we begin with ourselves as the starting point, rather than with God, there are only preferences based on each person's perception of reality. Nothing is accepted as objective truth. In this worldview, we're accountable to no one, life has no real purpose or meaning, there is no hope for our future beyond this life, no moral absolutes, and truth becomes relative and changeable. There is no sure foundation upon which to rest anything with that philosophy.

Atheists love to borrow from a Biblical worldview to identify what they consider good or evil or to make their case for justice or injustice. But in a world where "survival of the fittest" is the name of the game, what is advantageous to me may not be in your best interest and vice versa. If we came into existence through mere chance and time, how can our lives or the lives of others have any intrinsic value? We're all just "cosmic accidents" trying to make the most of this random existence. Deep inside we know this is not true. We inherently know that life does have value and meaning and that we were created *on* purpose and *for* a purpose.

That brings us to the Bible's answer to the question "How did we get here?" Scripture opens with that answer from the first verse:

In the beginning God created the heavens and the earth. (Genesis 1:1)

The New Testament book of Hebrews tells us that He did so by the power of His Word:

By faith we understand that the universe was created by the word of God, so that what is seen was not made out of things that are visible. (Hebrews 11:3, ESV)

The rest of Genesis 1 goes on to detail God's creation, culminating in man and woman, the pinnacle of His design:

Then God said, "Let Us make man in Our image, according to Our likeness; and let them rule over the fish of the sea and over the birds of the sky and over the cattle and over all the earth, and over every creeping thing that creeps on the earth." God created man in His own image, in the image of God He created him; male and female He created them. (Genesis 1:26-27)

Humans are so special and unique in God's creation that after giving an overview in Genesis 1, chapter 2 explains His process in greater detail. Isn't it exciting to know that an all-powerful God cared enough to create us in His image and give us dominion over all His other creatures? How much more purpose and value can one have than that? An all-knowing, all-loving, and all-wise God chose to specifically create you and me as male or female human beings with inherent worth merely because He purposed to bring us into existence. With a Biblical worldview, we all have value because we are made in the image of God. We have a purpose greater than ourselves with a future hope of a blissful eternity. It also means we live in a world filled with moral absolutes, a system of justice in which evil does not prevail, and truth is an unchanging foundation upon which to build our lives.

But that leads us to the next big question of life, "Why?"—or more specifically, "Why are we here?"

Why Are We Here?

The Bible tells us that we were ultimately created for God's glory:

"Worthy are You, our Lord and our God, to receive glory and honor and power; for You created all things, and because of Your will they existed and were created." (Revelation 4:11)

The *Westminster Shorter Catechism* is a series of questions and answers that teach the basic doctrines of Christianity. One of its most well-known questions is #1: "What is the chief end of man?" The answer confirms what Scripture says declaring, "Man's chief end is to glorify God and to enjoy Him forever." When we realize we were created both by God and for God, that truth helps life make sense. He created us to showcase His love, power, and glory, and we are the beneficiaries of His plan both for this life and for all eternity. Knowing that our purpose is to love and live for God puts all we do into context and perspective as we live for someone and something higher than ourselves.

I have heard objections from atheists and God-haters claiming He is an egotistical, maniacal being who needs us to validate and praise Him with our devotion and obedience. This is a completely erroneous, and ironically arrogant, view because first of all, God doesn't *need* anything, especially not from us. On the contrary, it was out of His selfless love that He chose to create us and bestow His generous love on us. If He is the supreme being above all of creation that ever was or ever will be—which He is—then isn't it the ultimate act of love to share Himself with us? It is profoundly generous and gracious for Him to bring us into existence to point us to the source of perfect love and all that is good. Then, to think that He asks us to join Him in a relationship not only for this temporal life but for all of eternity—what could be better than that? Yes, He is God and gets all the glory, and He deserves all of our obedience and praise because He alone is worthy. But nothing could be in our higher interest! That leads us to our next big question of life that the Bible answers for us—how should we live?

How Do We Live While We Are Here?

Would you be surprised if I said the Bible isn't a rule book for life?

Maybe you've seen the acronym:

B—basic

I—instructions

B—before

L—leaving

E—earth

While this is technically true because the Bible gives us all we need for life and godliness (see 2 Peter 1:3), it is ultimately a book about God and His plan of redemption through Jesus and how we fit into that plan. It's about who God is, what He is like, what He has done, and what He will do. And yes, it is also about what He wants us to do.

Once again, the Bible tells us how and what that looks like:

For we are His workmanship, created in Christ Jesus for good works, which God prepared beforehand so that we would walk in them. (Ephesians 2:10)

We were created for "good works" that God prepared for us to do. This shows us He has a plan and purpose for each of our lives. When we live guided by the Holy Spirit through God's Word, we will naturally do good as an outflow of our relationship with Him. This does not mean those works help us attain heaven because we could never do enough to earn salvation. God clarifies exactly what those "good works" are and what it is that He requires of us—and that is faith in His Son, our Lord and Savior, Jesus Christ:

Jesus answered and said to them, "This is the work of God, that you believe in Him whom He has sent." (John 6:29)

This is because we are saved by grace alone, through faith alone, in Jesus alone—not by our deeds or behavior as Ephesians tells us:

For by grace you have been saved through faith; and that not of yourselves, it is the gift of God; not as a result of works, so that no one may boast. (Ephesians 2:8-9)

As John 6:29 tells us, our primary job in this life is to believe in Jesus who was sent by God to rescue us from this sinful, fallen world. The Greek word used for "believe," has the connotation of trust, which we do when we no longer try to work our way to heaven but trust Christ alone for salvation. It is not just an intellectual assent because even the demons believe in Jesus:

You believe that God is one. You do well; the demons also believe, and shudder. (James 2:19)

By living in close fellowship with Him through His Word and prayer, He will guide us along the path we should take until He calls us home to be with Him forever as the Bible tells us:

You guide me with your counsel, and afterward you will receive me to glory. Whom have I in heaven but you? And there is nothing on earth that I desire besides you. (Psalm 73:24-25, ESV)

God has also included some practical guidelines for living here as we await Christ's return or His calling us home. He has a purpose for each of us, but the Bible doesn't specifically tell us the exact details of how that should look. It does not contain direct answers for every situation or decision we face. You've probably noticed that no specific verses tell us who to marry or what career to pursue. Instead, it gives overarching principles that, through wisdom, prayer, and the guidance of the Holy Spirit, lead us on the right path and aid us in making wise, God-honoring decisions. It helps us ask questions and make well-reasoned choices in every area of life. One of the first questions we should ask ourselves is, "Does this bring God glory?"

Whether, then, you eat or drink or whatever you do, do all to the glory of God. (1 Corinthians 10:31)

One of our primary purposes is to reflect God's love and light in this world where darkness is often present, so others may see Him in us and be drawn to Him as well. We do this when we live in such a way as to honor Him and love others as He loves us.

The closer we stay to God in His Word and prayer, the better we will know Him—what He likes and doesn't like, what brings Him glory and honor, and what dishonors Him. This makes it easier to know which choice to make or which path to take:

Your word is a lamp to my feet and a light to my path. (Psalm 119:105)

This leads us to some other questions to consider, including whether each choice or decision will further God's work on earth, multiply the talents and gifts He has given us, or make the best use of our time:

Therefore be careful how you walk, not as unwise men but as wise, making the most of your time, because the days are evil. (Ephesians 5:15-16)

In the Gospel of Matthew, chapter 25:14-30, Jesus tells a parable of a nobleman who traveled to a distant country. Before he left, he called three of his servants and entrusted each with a portion of money to do business with until he returned. Upon his homecoming, he took an accounting of each one's work, praising and rewarding those who had wisely invested and increased their master's assets. Yet one servant who feared his master hid the money and did nothing with it. He did not even put it into the bank where it could have earned interest. The master was distraught with the lazy servant, took away the portion he had entrusted to him, and cast him away.

This shows us that God does not ask anything from us unless He first supplies all we need to accomplish His will. He has gifted each of us with talents, abilities, and resources to use for our well-being and the benefit of others and ultimately for His glory. Once again, this gives purpose and meaning to all that we have and all that we do.

Whatever path we choose, we have all been given an assignment from Jesus before He returned to Heaven after His resurrection. Whether we work in a hospital or a factory, at home or abroad, there is one job we all have in common, and that is to share the Gospel—the good news that Jesus saves! This command that Jesus gave us is often called "The Great Commission" which we see here:

And Jesus came and said to them, "All authority in heaven and on earth has been given to me. Go therefore and make disciples of all nations, baptizing them in the name of the Father and of the Son and of the Holy Spirit, teaching them to observe all that I have commanded you. And behold, I am with you always, to the end of the age." (Matthew 28:18-20, ESV)

God doesn't *need* us to do any of His work, but He has given us the privilege and responsibility to partner with Him in it. What an awesome calling and honor! Not only does sharing the Gospel glorify God, but it shows our faith in a message so important that we want others to know it so they, too, can be saved and enjoy a restored relationship with our creator!

Penn Jillette of the famous magician duo, Penn and Teller, and a staunch atheist, surprisingly admitted the importance of evangelizing and the care it shows for others when he stated he doesn't respect people who don't proselytize. This was his reasoning:

"I don't respect that at all. If you believe that there's a heaven and hell and people could be going to hell or not getting eternal life or whatever, and you think that it's not really worth telling them this because it would make it socially awkward, and atheists who think that people shouldn't proselytize — 'Just leave me alone, keep your religion to yourself.'

"How much do you have to hate somebody to not proselytize?" Jillette asked. "How much do you have to hate somebody to believe that everlasting life is possible and not tell them that? If I believed beyond a shadow of a doubt that a truck was coming at you and you didn't believe it, and that truck was bearing down on you, there's a certain point where I tackle you. And this is more important than that."[10]

So, there you have it—our basic instructions before leaving Earth include:

---

[10] Erin Roach, "ATHEISM: Penn Jillette urges evangelism," Baptist Press, February 12, 2009, https://www.baptistpress.com/resource-library/news/atheism-penn-jillette-urges-evangelism/.

1. B—Believe in the Lord Jesus Christ.
2. I—In His Word and prayer, walk closely with God to discern His will for your life.
3. B—Be diligent to make the most of every opportunity to use your time, talents, and treasures to further His kingdom.
4. L—Let all you do glorify God.
5. E—Evangelize and share the Gospel wherever you are and whenever you can.

This verse sums it up best:

But seek first His kingdom and His righteousness, and all these things will be added to you. (Matthew 6:33)

So, now that we know how to live while we are here, what's next?

Where Are We Going?

Now that we've established how we came to be here, why we are here, and how we should live while we're here, it only makes sense to ask, "What's next?"

Of course, all of the previous material has hinted at the answer to this all-important question, but let's give it some more detailed attention. We know this life is temporary as none of us make it out alive, so knowing what lies ahead should be one of our greatest concerns.

It's been said there are only two certainties in life: death and taxes. While this is a humorous yet pessimistic view, these matters are definite realities we all face. The Bible tells us that each of us will one day perish and give an accounting to our creator:

And inasmuch as it is appointed for men to die once and after this comes judgment. (Hebrews 9:27)

Yet the reality of that truth does not have to be as foreboding, or terrifying, as we may think. Jesus Himself gave us a much more optimistic picture, filled with mansions when He described our future destination:

Let not your heart be troubled: ye believe in God, believe also in me. In my Father's house are many mansions: if it were not so, I would have told you. I go to prepare a place for you. And if I go and prepare a place for you, I will come again, and receive you unto myself; that where I am, there ye may be also. (John 14:1-3)

Paul, in his letter to the Corinthians, encouraged believers that even if we would lose all that we own including our very lives, we have a blessed hope in Heaven:

For we know that if the earthly tent which is our house is torn down, we have a building from God, a house not made with hands, eternal in the heavens. (2 Corinthians 5:1)

The Bible gives us numerous verses that confirm what we all know deep inside—that there must be more to life than what we see or experience here, and that there must be something after this, such as:

For indeed in this house we groan, longing to be clothed with our dwelling from heaven. (2 Corinthians 5:2)

Inherently we know our souls are eternal and that we don't just exist for this short time while we are here on earth and then return to nothingness. When a loved one dies, we comfort ourselves and others with sentiments such as, "They are in a better place," "They're no longer suffering," and "May they rest in peace."

As far back as the earliest times, people have longed for eternal bliss, free of the pain, sorrow, toil, and death that this fallen world offers. We long to return to the perfect state in which we began before sin entered and cursed this existence. This verse in Hebrews refers to the early Israelites who looked forward to an eternal home with God:

But as it is, they desire a better country, that is, a heavenly one. Therefore God is not ashamed to be called their God; for He has prepared a city for them. (Hebrews 11:16)

The book of Revelation tells of our glorious future when Jesus returns and a new heaven and earth are established:

Then I saw a new heaven and a new earth; for the first heaven and the first earth passed away, and there is no longer any sea. And I saw the holy city, new Jerusalem, coming down out of heaven from God, made ready as a bride adorned for her husband. And I heard a loud voice from the throne, saying, "Behold, the tabernacle of God is among men, and He will dwell among them, and they shall be His people, and God Himself will be among them, and He will wipe away every tear from their eyes; and there will no longer be any death; there will no longer be any mourning, or crying, or pain; the first things have passed away." (Revelation 21:1-4)

What a hopeful future! Knowing that someday, a perfect eternity awaits us gives us hope in even the darkest times.

But, does everyone go to this eternal place of paradise? In the Gospel of Matthew, Jesus lists two possible destinations, and the second is the complete opposite of unending joy and happiness:

"These will go away into eternal punishment, but the righteous into eternal life." (Matthew 25:46)

So, that begs the next question, if only the righteous inherit eternal life, "How do I get there?"

How Do I Get There?

As noted earlier, once we die, we face judgment and must give an account of our lives before our creator. Of course, each of us knows there are deep recesses of our hearts and lives we'd rather not talk about—or worse yet, be exposed to have judged. We'd rather rationalize our sins and shame by comparing ourselves to others with claims of, "I'm not as bad as...," or "Everyone does it," or even, "Well, I've never murdered anyone."

But the problem with this assessment is that it is wholly inadequate. Our standard isn't other people, and God doesn't "grade on a curve." His standard for entry into heaven is perfection. Because He is holy and perfect, not one single sin can exist in His presence. Therefore, the Bible tells us that if we have broken even one of God's laws, we are wholly guilty before Him:

For whoever keeps the whole law and yet stumbles in one point, he has become guilty of all. (James 2:10)

At first glance, this seems to be troubling news, considering no one is perfect, which means nobody qualifies for heaven or eternal life. The Bible confirms that not one of us is righteous:

As it is written, there is none righteous, no, not one. (Romans 3:10, KJV)

Yet, the fact that none of us are righteous is actually wonderful news! Since nobody is perfect, yet God's requirement for entry into heaven is perfection, there must be another way. Thankfully, there is! Pastor and author Adrian Rogers said, "God doesn't grade on a curve, He grades on the cross." When God created the world and placed the first man and woman in the perfect garden, He knew they would choose to follow their own will and rebel against their creator, just as we all have done ever since. But in His divine providence, He also provided a solution and promised a savior. Immediately after the fall of man into sin, God revealed His plan for our redemption in the coming of a Messiah to rescue us.

The Israelites looked ahead to their deliverer throughout history, and the entire Old Testament tells the story of God's chosen people through whom the Messiah would come. Prophets and prophecies detailed this coming until the fullness of time when a baby, born of a virgin, arrived in Bethlehem that first Christmas night:

Joseph also went up from Galilee, from the city of Nazareth, to Judea, to the city of David which is called Bethlehem, because he was of the house and family of David, in order to register along with Mary, who was engaged to him, and was with child. While they were there, the days were completed for her to give birth. And she gave birth to her firstborn son; and she wrapped Him in cloths, and laid Him in a manger, because there was no room for them in the inn. (Luke 2:4-7)

For a child will be born to us, a son will be given to us; And the government will rest on His shoulders; And His name will be called Wonderful Counselor, Mighty God, Eternal Father, Prince of Peace. (Isaiah 9:6)

But as for you, Bethlehem Ephrathah, too little to be among the clans of Judah, from you One will go forth for Me to be ruler in Israel. His goings forth are from long ago, from the days of eternity." (Micah 5:2)

That is why we say the Bible is ultimately a book about God and His plan to redeem us through our Lord Jesus Christ. No other religion has a God who did what was needed for us to have salvation, other than Jesus. The Gospels of Matthew, Mark, Luke, and John detail His life and work, culminating in His death and resurrection, and finally His ascension into heaven.

The Old Testament Jews, as they awaited the Messiah, were given the Law, which included the Ten Commandments and an elaborate system of worship and sacrifice to seek God's forgiveness for breaking those commands. Yet those sacrifices were insufficient to fully atone for the people's sins. They were merely a foreshadowing of the ultimate, once-for-all sacrifice of the Lamb of God who would take away our sins completely and forever. Hebrews 10:4-10 tells us:

For it is impossible for the blood of bulls and goats to take away sins. Therefore, when He comes into the world, He says,

"SACRIFICE AND OFFERING YOU HAVE NOT DESIRED,
BUT A BODY YOU HAVE PREPARED FOR ME;
IN WHOLE BURNT OFFERINGS AND sacrifices FOR SIN YOU
HAVE TAKEN NO PLEASURE.
"THEN I SAID, 'BEHOLD, I HAVE COME

(IN THE SCROLL OF THE BOOK IT IS WRITTEN OF ME) TO DO YOUR WILL, O GOD.'"

After saying above, "SACRIFICES AND OFFERINGS AND WHOLE BURNT OFFERINGS AND sacrifices FOR SIN YOU HAVE NOT DESIRED, NOR HAVE YOU TAKEN PLEASURE in them" (which are offered according to the Law), then He said, "BEHOLD, I HAVE COME TO DO YOUR WILL." He takes away the first in order to establish the second. By this will we have been sanctified through the offering of the body of Jesus Christ once for all.

Did you see that last verse? It is the key to understanding the answer to our question, "How do we get there?" If none of us is good enough to go to heaven on our own merits, we must look to one who is. Jesus told us that He is "the way" to the Father:

Jesus said to him, "I am the way, and the truth, and the life; no one comes to the Father but through Me." (John 14:6)

He lived a perfect, sinless life that we never could, which qualified Him to take all of our sins to the cross, where they were crucified with Him. He died, was buried, and rose again to new life, defeating sin and death forever. Because His work was finished on the cross, our salvation is secure when we trust Him alone to save us. Through faith in Christ, our sins are removed and replaced with His righteousness which is credited to us:

*That if you confess with your mouth Jesus as Lord,
and believe in your heart that God raised Him from
the dead, you will be saved; for with the heart a person
believes, resulting in righteousness, and with the
mouth he confesses, resulting in salvation. (Romans
10:9-10)*

This makes us "the righteous" who can inherit eternal
life!

We've covered a lot of ground in this chapter, but as you
can see, the Bible answers all of life's major questions
including: "How did we get here?", "Why are we here?",
"How should we live?", "Where are we going?", and
"How do we get there?"

Knowing the answers to these questions gives life
purpose and direction and helps life make sense!

Chapter 5: The Problem of Evil

For we do not wrestle against flesh and blood, but against the rulers, against the authorities, against the cosmic powers over this present darkness, against the spiritual forces of evil in the heavenly places. (Ephesians 6:12, ESV)

It's no surprise that almost every book or movie plot portrays some form of battle between good and evil. Whether it's an obvious hero versus villain story or a more subtle battle of someone triumphing in the face of adversity, wickedness is an ever-present element in our lives. That brings us to another monumental question of life "Why is there evil and suffering in the world?"

Why Do Evil and Suffering Exist?

To fully address this question, we must go back to Chapter 4 and add some details. There we looked at how we got here and why we're here, being created by God to glorify Him and enjoy Him forever. As the culmination of His creation, He gave us dominion over all other creatures on earth. But ultimately, we are accountable to Him.

However, before humans even existed, the Bible tells us that a clash for authority occurred between Himself and His created angels when the devil sought to take God's glory and reign in His place:

How you have fallen from heaven, O star of the morning, son of the dawn! You have been cut down to the earth, You who have weakened the nations! But you said in your heart, 'I will ascend to heaven; I will raise my throne above the stars of God, And I will sit on the mount of assembly In the recesses of the north. I will ascend above the heights of the clouds; I will make myself like the Most High.' Nevertheless you will be thrust down to Sheol, To the recesses of the pit. (Isaiah 14:12-15)

Because God is holy, perfect, powerful, and sovereign over all, it is only right that He not share His glory with anyone or anything less than Himself. Even the devil, a created being and fallen angel, is subject to God's authority. (For more on this topic, see Ezekiel 28:11-19, where a prophecy about the King of Tyre parallels the devil's downfall.)

It Started with Sin

Shortly after the creation account, the devil appeared to man in an attempt to bring others with him in his rebellion against God:

Now the serpent was more crafty than any beast of the field which the LORD God had made. And he said to the woman, "Indeed, has God said, 'You shall not eat from any tree of the garden'?" The woman said to the serpent, "From the fruit of the trees of the garden we may eat; but from the fruit of the tree which is in the middle of the garden, God has said, 'You shall not eat from it or touch it, or you will die.'" The serpent said to the woman, "You surely will not die! For God knows that in the day you eat from it your eyes will be opened, and you will be like God, knowing good and evil." (Genesis 3:1-5)

Not only did the devil begin by getting Eve to distrust God and His Word—a tactic he still uses on us today, he also appealed to her pride by telling her that she could "be like God." It was a difficult offer to refuse, and she did not:

When the woman saw that the tree was good for food, and that it was a delight to the eyes, and that the tree was desirable to make one wise, she took from its fruit and ate; and she gave also to her husband with her, and he ate. (Genesis 3:6)

Taking the forbidden fruit and eating it, against God's direct command, Adam and Eve fell into sin and set a cascade of events into motion that would affect the entire human race to come, including you and me:

Then the eyes of both of them were opened, and they knew that they were naked; and they sewed fig leaves together and made themselves loin coverings. (Genesis 3:7)

Suddenly, their eyes were opened to know evil rather than only the good they had previously experienced. From that point on, man would no longer enjoy a perfect creation or live in unbroken fellowship with God. For He had warned them:

The LORD God commanded the man, saying, "From any tree of the garden you may eat freely; but from the tree of the knowledge of good and evil you shall not eat, for in the day that you eat from it you will surely die." (Genesis 2:16-17)

God does not place arbitrary restrictions on us to limit us or dampen our enjoyment of life but to protect us so we experience only His best, just as a loving parent should. When we think we know better or refuse to obey His authority, we may experience momentary pleasure, but we also set ourselves up for potentially evil or harmful consequences.

Adam and Eve did not immediately experience physical death, but they were subject to spiritual death and separation from God. The perfect fellowship between God and man was broken, and ever since each of us has inherited Adam's sinful nature:

Behold, I was brought forth in iniquity, and in sin my mother conceived me. (Psalm 51:5)

As evil entered God's perfect world through man's rebellion against Him, He informed them that the consequences of disobedience would include increased pain in childbirth, a struggle for authority between men and women, ongoing toil in our work, pain, suffering, and eventually the physical death of our mortal bodies. (See more in Genesis 3:14-19.)

Yet, once again, even in this dismal outlook, God shows mercy and compassion as He gives a foreshadowing of the sacrifice that would cover our sins:

The LORD God made garments of skin for Adam and his wife, and clothed them. (Genesis 3:21)

An animal was sacrificed to provide a covering for their shame and nakedness, which foreshadowed the Lamb of God that would take away sins forever.

Physical death was actually an act of mercy as God did not want us to end up in this predicament of living in a fallen world forever. For our protection, He sent Adam and Eve from the garden and away from access to the tree of life that would have given them the potential to live forever in this fallen state:

Then the LORD God said, "Behold, the man has become like one of Us, knowing good and evil; and now, he might stretch out his hand, and take also from the tree of life, and eat, and live forever"— therefore the LORD God sent him out from the garden of Eden, to cultivate the ground from which he was taken. So He drove the man out; and at the east of the garden of Eden He stationed the cherubim and the flaming sword which turned every direction to guard the way to the tree of life. (Genesis 3:22-24)

Now, death brings us new life as we are born again through faith in Jesus. The old self, marred by sin, has been crucified with Christ. We have the hope of eternal life, raised again with Him when this earthly life is done. Because of His sacrifice on our behalf, we will be fully restored to perfection and unbroken fellowship with God again as it was always meant to be.

But you may protest, Adam and Eve sinned—not me. So, why am I included in the curse of this fallen world? God tells us that through that one man, sin entered the world, and we are all born with an inclination to sin:

Therefore, just as through one man sin entered into the world, and death through sin, and so death spread to all men, because all sinned. (Romans 5:12)

Not one of us goes a single day, or even a single hour, without sinning in some way. Left to ourselves, we will default to do what pleases us first. Even in a perfect world with optimal circumstances in the Garden of Eden, man still chose to sin and act according to his own will rather than obey God. The book of Judges, chapter 21, tells of a time when God's people had no king, and instead of following God, *"everyone did what was right in their own eyes."* Lawlessness reigned. People decided for themselves what they believed to be right or wrong, and morality was relative. Everyone lived according to their own "truth." Sounds similar to today, doesn't it?

Whether subtle sins of pride, hidden sins like lust, or more obvious sins such as dishonesty or adultery, our hearts are bent toward putting ourselves and our wants and desires before God and others. If the greatest commandments are to love God above all and love others as ourselves as Matthew 22:36-40 tells us, which of us can claim to have never broken these? The world tells us to "follow our hearts," and to "love ourselves," but the Bible confirms we cannot trust our hearts because they are desperately wicked:

The heart is deceitful above all things, and desperately sick; who can understand it? (Jeremiah 17:9, ESV)

Man is no longer "basically good" since the fall into sin in the garden long ago. Man is not even morally neutral. Jesus told us this when He said:

And He was saying, "That which proceeds out of the man, that is what defiles the man. For from within, out of the heart of men, proceed the evil thoughts, fornications, thefts, murders, adulteries, deeds of coveting and wickedness, as well as deceit, sensuality, envy, slander, pride and foolishness. All these evil things proceed from within and defile the man." (Mark 7:20-23)

Even Christians, who have the Holy Spirit living inside us to help us carry out God's will, still wrestle with sin as long as we are in these mortal, fleshly bodies. The apostle Paul detailed the struggle with which we can all relate:

For what I am doing, I do not understand; for I am not practicing what I would like to do, but I am doing the very thing I hate. But if I do the very thing I do not want to do, I agree with the Law, confessing that the Law is good. So now, no longer am I the one doing it, but sin which dwells in me. For I know that nothing good dwells in me, that is, in my flesh; for the willing is present in me, but the doing of the good is not. For the good that I want, I do not do, but I practice the very evil that I do not want. But if I am doing the very thing I do not want, I am no longer the one doing it, but sin which dwells in me. (Romans 7:15-20)

When someone asks, "Why does God allow bad things to happen to good people?" The answer to that question is that it only happened once—to Jesus Christ. There are no truly good people. Only God is good, as the Bible tells us:

As it is written: "None is righteous, no, not one." (Romans 3:10)

And Jesus said to him, "Why do you call Me good? No one is good except God alone." (Mark 10:18)

Because Jesus was crucified yet had committed no sin, this was truly the only time something bad happened to a good person. Unless all people trust Christ for salvation and have their minds transformed by the Holy Spirit through His Word, the world's problems will never be fully solved.

From the beginning of time, humans battled in the clash for authority with God as the devil did before he fell away. Will we submit to our loving Heavenly Father for our good and His glory, or will we seek our own way and attempt to be our own authority and in essence our own "god"?

It's been said that "Ever since God made man in His image, man has been returning the favor." We see it worldwide—people questioning Him and His Word and conforming Him into an image they can live with. Perhaps you've heard things like, "To me, God is..." or "My god would never..." And, in a way they are correct—their god would never... because their god doesn't exist! The battle for control between God and man is as old as time and is the main reason evil exists in this world today as people put themselves before God and others:

What is the source of quarrels and conflicts among you? Is not the source your pleasures that wage war in your members? You lust and do not have; so you commit murder. You are envious and cannot obtain; so you fight and quarrel. You do not have because you do not ask. You ask and do not receive, because you ask with wrong motives, so that you may spend it on your pleasures. You adulteresses, do you not know that friendship with the world is hostility toward God?

Therefore whoever wishes to be a friend of the world makes himself an enemy of God. (James 4:1-4)

Jesus even warned that this world would bring us trouble, especially as His followers. But we could take comfort in knowing He has overcome the world and evil will one day be abolished forever:

"These things I have spoken to you, so that in Me you may have peace. In the world you have tribulation, but take courage; I have overcome the world." (John 16:33)

But if God created us to be His special people to love and be loved and to have fellowship with Him, why does He allow evil in the first place?

Why Does God Allow Evil?

This age-old question is one of the most commonly asked about God. It started in the Garden of Eden when man disobeyed God and ate from the Tree of the Knowledge of Good and Evil. You could say man chose to know evil by this act of rebellion. For us to freely love God, He also created us with the ability to *not* love and follow Him. Yet, we still ask why God allowed it, knowing we would make that choice.

However, that question implies a couple of things... First, if God allows evil and could stop it, is He even good? Or if He allowed it because He couldn't stop it, then is He all-powerful? Yet, neither of these options exists because we know He *is* all-good—perfectly holy and hating evil. We also know He is the mighty, omnipotent one who created everything. So, then what is the reason for it? Because He is also all-knowing, or omniscient, we know He must have reasons for allowing evil to be part of His master plan. He knows what we cannot know and sees every aspect of every situation. It has been said that if we could see the specific details of any scenario as God sees it, we would respond exactly the same way He does. It is comforting to know that He is our wise Father and that His thoughts and deeds are always greater than ours:

"For My thoughts are not your thoughts, nor are your ways My ways," declares the LORD. For as the heavens are higher than the earth, so are My ways higher than your ways and My thoughts than your thoughts." (Isaiah 55:8-9)

Before we delve into the many possible reasons God allowed evil to exist, we need to acknowledge that anyone who is truly suffering is not going to be comforted by intellectual or philosophical explanations for the existence of evil in the world. But, the hope of Christianity gives comfort and confidence that no other worldview offers and reminds us that this world is not all there is. God has promised us a perfect eternal future where pain, tears, and suffering no longer exist. In Jesus Christ, we have a future expectation that can help us through even the darkest times. At the cross, Jesus ultimately defeated death and evil forever.

Anything we encounter here is temporary, no matter how difficult:

For momentary, light affliction is producing for us an eternal weight of glory far beyond all comparison, while we look not at the things which are seen, but at the things which are not seen; for the things which are seen are temporal, but the things which are not seen are eternal. (2 Corinthians 4:17-18)

Even though these earthly trials are temporary in the spectrum of eternity, they can still be challenging to handle or even tragic as we experience suffering here. But God offers a promise that can help us endure, and that is His assurance that He will work all things for good for those who love Him:

And we know that God causes all things to work together for good to those who love God, to those who are called according to His purpose. (Romans 8:28)

That may include circumstances that turn out favorably, or it could mean that the trials will work to refine or strengthen our faith as we trust in God through them. It may mean spiritual growth as we see God working in our lives. Or, we may not even see the good God is bringing about from our situation here on earth but rather receive the good as eternal rewards. He is always working towards our sanctification as He makes us more like His Son, our Lord Jesus Christ, and prepares us for eternity with Him. This is one of the key components of how a Biblical worldview makes life make sense. Trusting God to work all things for good and keeping an eternal perspective puts everything we see, do, and experience here into its proper place. This life is merely a preparation and training for a blissful eternity with our Lord and Savior.

But that still leaves us asking, "Why do we have to endure it here?"

What if Everything Was Perfect?

It might help to first consider, what if there was no evil in the world? How would we truly know what good is if we had no comparison? Have you ever been seriously ill and then realized how amazing it feels to be healthy? That is something we can easily take for granted. We have a newfound appreciation for what is good and right when things are terribly wrong.

The same can be said about love. How often do we genuinely appreciate the love of others until it is tested or tried? Love that is coerced or forced is no love at all.

God's Love is Displayed

As contradictory as it may sound, allowing evil into the world was one of the greatest ways God could demonstrate both His infinite goodness and the depth of His love. By letting us see just how horrible sin and suffering can be, we can also see just how far He would go to prove His love for us. Not only did He come and partake of the worst of that suffering Himself, He did it to rescue us from it. The Bible confirms that Jesus did this because His motive was love:

"I have been crucified with Christ; and it is no longer I who live, but Christ lives in me; and the life which I now live in the flesh I live by faith in the Son of God, who loved me and gave Himself up for me. (Galatians 2:20)

He doesn't allow anything to happen to us that He wasn't willing to endure Himself, and He can empathize with us because He understands our pain.

God's Goodness is Showcased

Evil in this world also showcases how exemplary God is when contrasted with how horrific evil is. Because there is bad, I know what good is. To see the brilliance of a diamond, the jeweler sets it against a black cloth. We see the magnificence, power, and glory of God when we realize He is lifting us out of the darkness of this world and into His marvelous light to live with Him forever:

But you are a chosen race, a royal priesthood, a holy nation, a people for his own possession, that you may proclaim the excellencies of him who called you out of darkness into his marvelous light. (1 Peter 2:9, ESV)

We Have Eternal Hope

A third reason for the existence of evil in this world is that it makes us long for our eternal home. As noted earlier, keeping an eternal perspective helps keep this life and all of its challenges in their proper perspective. It doesn't mean every trial will be painless, but knowing that our suffering is temporary alleviates some of the burden and gives us hope for a brighter future:

And after you have suffered a little while, the God of all grace, who has called you to his eternal glory in Christ, will himself restore, confirm, strengthen, and establish you. (1 Peter 5:10, ESV)

We Are Drawn to Jesus

Another reason God allows evil to exist for a time is that it draws us to Jesus—to rescue, save, heal, restore, and protect us. We look to Him to provide for all of our needs as we seek Him in prayer and His Word.

Maybe you've seen this in your own life—when circumstances are going well, we tend to neglect time with God and forget to pray and praise Him for all His blessings. Then, when trouble strikes, we often call out to Him for help. This pattern was repeated time and again throughout the Old Testament. God blessed His people abundantly, yet they forgot Him or worse abandoned Him to chase after other gods and worldly pleasures. He allowed hardship to come to bring them back to Him again and again. Human nature hasn't changed with time.

We Are Sanctified

But that gives us another reason why there is evil in this world—to sanctify us. This means that through our experiences, God works to make us more like His perfect Son, Jesus. A caring parent will allow certain circumstances and consequences in a child's life to teach them for their ultimate good:

And have you forgotten the exhortation that addresses you as sons? "My son, do not regard lightly the discipline of the Lord, nor be weary when reproved by Him. For the Lord disciplines the one He loves, and chastises every son whom He receives." It is for discipline that you have to endure. God is treating you as sons. For what son is there whom his father does not discipline? If you are left without discipline, in which all have participated, then you are illegitimate children and not sons. Besides this, we have had earthly fathers who disciplined us and we respected them. Shall we not much more be subject to the Father of spirits and live? For they disciplined us for a short time as it seemed best to them, but He disciplines us for our good, that we may share His holiness. For the moment all discipline seems painful rather than pleasant, but later it yields the peaceful fruit of righteousness to those who have been trained by it. (Hebrews 12:5-11, ESV)

We can take comfort knowing that He sees the big picture, while we don't. I once gave an example to someone struggling with this concept. He was a concerned father who was limiting his young son's electronic screen time so he would pursue more meaningful activities. If his son had his way, he would play video games from breakfast until bedtime. Although the young boy saw this limit as arbitrary and felt that his dad was unfairly restricting him from enjoying his favorite pastime, his dad acted in his best interest, despite how his son viewed the situation.

God tells us to trust Him like a child trusts their father, and nothing helps us exercise that more readily than when we experience pain or hardship. That's why we can rely on Him even when we don't fully understand Him.

We have little problem placing our lives into the care of a skilled airline pilot without knowing the first thing about how to operate the plane's controls or even about the pilot himself. Yet God, who has revealed Himself to us through His Word and who has created all, sees all, and knows all is even more worthy of our complete trust. As His children, we know He is a loving and perfect Father, who gives us what we need. Everything He does is for our eternal good and His glory:

He who did not spare His own Son, but delivered Him over for us all, how will He not also with Him freely give us all things? (Romans 8:32)

What's the Solution? (Hint: The Gospel)

Now that we've seen many reasons why God allowed evil into the world, how do we deal with it while we are here? Better yet, how do we overcome it? What's the solution? In one simple, yet extremely profound answer: the Gospel of our Lord Jesus Christ!

At the cross, Jesus defeated sin, death, and the power of the devil once and for all. His sacrifice paid the full price for our sins, and His perfect, righteous life earned us right standing with God and eternal happiness with Him.

The battles we face here are against a defeated foe. The Bible tells us that our battles with evil here are spiritual battles at their core:

For our struggle is not against flesh and blood, but against the rulers, against the powers, against the world forces of this darkness, against the spiritual forces of wickedness in the heavenly places. (Ephesians 6:12)

Our true enemies aren't other people, made of flesh and blood, but the evil forces at work in the world. As noted earlier, sin and evil came on the scene when man chose to rebel against God rather than submit to His authority. Therefore, as we place our faith and trust in Jesus and let Him rule as Lord of our lives, He gives us the grace and strength needed to fight against our sinful flesh and overcome the temptations we face each day.

He fills us with His Holy Spirit who guides us into all truth and turns our hearts towards Him so that we want to live according to His will rather than our own.

Imagine a world where everyone lived in the power of God's love and grace rather than seeking to fulfill our own pursuits and selfish desires. Evil would no longer have a place here. That is the ultimate result of Jesus's finished work on the cross. He is making everything new, and one day that will be our eternal reality! Jesus has already won the victory on our behalf:

"These things I have spoken to you, so that in Me you may have peace. In the world you have tribulation, but take courage; I have overcome the world." (John 16:33)

Because we are in Him, we too are overcomers:

But in all these things we overwhelmingly conquer through Him who loved us. (Romans 8:37)

So, take heart! We are on the winning side! God is in control, even when our lives sometimes seem out of control. We can trust that He is working all things for our good and His glory. We can take comfort in knowing that life on Earth is not all there is; it is just a tiny blip on the spectrum of eternity. He promises that anything we face here pales compared to the glorious future awaiting us in Him.

God's Word helps us keep an eternal perspective with our eyes focused on Him and our hearts trusting in His promises. It also gives us yet another reason that the Bible helps make life make sense!

Section Three

The Bible Makes Life Make Sense

Chapter 6: Relationships

For this reason I bow my knees before the Father, from whom every family in heaven and on earth derives its name. (Ephesians 3:14-15)

Until this point, we've looked at the many spiritual and intangible ways the Bible makes sense of life. But the Bible is also an extremely practical book that addresses all areas of our daily lives as we will explore in these final chapters. The Bible explains why we live as families rather than as lone individuals, why men and women marry, why we have fellowship and friendships, and why we learn, work, and rest. This chapter will explore our most important relationships and why they are so vital to our well-being.

The Concept of Family

The scope of this book is not large enough to include a detailed "how-to" on every area related to family relationships, nor is it meant to be a parenting manual. The concepts and truths taught throughout God's Word provide a solid foundation for both areas, and the purpose of this book is to show you how the Bible brings meaning to them.

The family unit is something we all share in some form, and those relationships can be some of our biggest sources of joy or our deepest sources of pain and sorrow. Interpersonal relations among family members can be complicated and problematic at times, yet can also be some of the closest, most precious relationships we share as we navigate the complexities of life.

But, why do we exist in family units rather than as individuals acting independently of one another? The Bible outlines the concept of this critical structure which has been the foundation and bedrock of society since the beginning of time.

Going back to the Garden of Eden, God created Adam and Eve with a mandate to be fruitful and multiply and fill the earth with children so that man would have dominion over the rest of His creation:

God blessed them; and God said to them, "Be fruitful and multiply, and fill the earth, and subdue it; and rule over the fish of the sea and over the birds of the sky and over every living thing that moves on the earth." (Genesis 1:28)

God began His design for the family when He brought man and woman together as one:

For this reason a man shall leave his father and his mother, and be joined to his wife; and they shall become one flesh. (Genesis 2:24)

Jesus repeated this design in the Gospel of Matthew:

He answered, "Have you not read that he who created them from the beginning made them male and female, and said, 'Therefore a man shall leave his father and his mother and hold fast to his wife, and the two shall become one flesh'? So they are no longer two but one flesh. What therefore God has joined together, let not man separate." (Matthew 19:4-6)

God created man in His image and adopted us as sons and daughters through His only begotten Son, our Lord Jesus Christ. He is our Father and we are His children. As believers, we are brothers and sisters in Christ and part of God's family.

From the beginning of creation, society has been structured this way, and studies show that strong families are beneficial for society to prosper. The inverse of that is also true. Just as evil is the absence of good, society crumbles in the presence of fractured families. God designed parents to care for and train their children in His ways just as He lovingly parents His children when we come to Him in faith. Parents are meant to teach them, guard them, and provide for their needs as God does for us:

Train up a child in the way he should go, even when he is old he will not depart from it. (Proverbs 22:6)

"Are not two sparrows sold for a cent? And yet not one of them will fall to the ground apart from your Father. But the very hairs of your head are all numbered. So

do not fear; you are more valuable than many sparrows." (Matthew 10:29-31)

Whenever there is a challenge to His design, problems are possible if not inevitable. Stable families provide love, care, support, safety, companionship, and a sense of belonging and community. We were not designed to manage life by ourselves, which is why one of God's greatest provisions is the gift of families. Here are a few more verses that show God's design for families:

Children, obey your parents in the Lord, for this is right. "Honor your father and mother" (this is the first commandment with a promise), "that it may go well with you and that you may live long in the land." Fathers, do not provoke your children to anger, but bring them up in the discipline and instruction of the Lord. (Ephesians 6:1-4, ESV)

When people live according to God's good design of father, mother, and children in close communion with Him, children not only survive but thrive.

Studies show the opposite is also true. Just a 10% increase in single-parent families leads to a 17% increase in juvenile crime.[11] According to the America First Policy Institute, fatherless children are 3 to 20 times more likely to be incarcerated than children

---

[11] "Effects of Fatherless Families on Crime Rates," Marripedia, accessed December 8, 2023, https://www.marripedia.org/effects_of_fatherless_families_on_crime_r ates.

raised in dual-parent households. Eighty-five percent of youth in prison have an absent father.[12] Seventy-one percent of teachers and 90% of law enforcement officials state that the lack of parental supervision at home is a major contributor to violence in schools. Children who feel closeness to their fathers are 80% less likely to spend time in jail. Girls raised without fathers are more likely to be sexually promiscuous as they seek love from the male figure in their lives they lack. Children from single-parent homes are more likely to:

- Commit suicide (5x)
- Drop out of high school (9x)
- Abuse drugs and alcohol (10x)
- Commit rape (14x)
- Run away from home (32x)[13]

The importance of fathers in families is evident considering we were created to have a relationship with our Heavenly Father, and it is clear why problems exist when either of these relationships are damaged or severed.

---

[12] "Fatherhood and Crime," America First Policy Institute, June 25, 2024, https://americafirstpolicy.com/issues/fact-sheet-fatherhood-and-crime.

[13] Sherry Palmer, "Fatherless Home Statistics," July 19, 2023, https://www.fixfamilycourts.com/divorce-child-custody-blog/single-mother-home-statistics/.

Of course, many single parents have found themselves in that situation through circumstances beyond their control, and this in no way points blame or guilt on them at all. Instead, it is only to illustrate how the effects of sin's curse on this fallen world have affected God's perfect plan for the family. By keeping families fractured, the enemy can wreak the havoc he so desires, once again showing that an absence of God leads only to pain and suffering.

It is often said that we can't fit a square peg into a round hole, and as the world tries to redefine what a family unit looks like, we move farther away from God's best for us. He set up His design and decrees for our good, and the family finds its structure in our relationship between us as His children and Him as our loving and perfect Father.

Marriage

For this reason a man shall leave his father and mother and shall be joined to his wife, and the two shall become one flesh. This mystery is great; but I am speaking with reference to Christ and the church. (Ephesians 5:31-32)

One of the other main relationships that have been the foundation of society since its inception is the marriage covenant between a man and a woman. The Bible also explains and makes sense of this union—not only why it is structured the way it is, but also its immense significance.

Just as God the Father designed our families to mirror His relationship with us, He also set apart man and woman to be in a special relationship as husband and wife, mirroring Christ's relationship with the church. As God's Son, Jesus came to earth to redeem a people for Himself, and as believers, we are His beloved. God likens our relationship with the Son to the marriage relationship between a husband and wife. Christ is the bridegroom, and the church is His bride.

That illustrates the profound significance of a Biblical marriage between a man and woman, and why only that form of union makes sense theologically. When lived out as a husband lovingly caring for his wife and a wife honoring her husband, the picture of the Gospel is displayed for the world to see. This topic is so significant that I wrote an entire book on the subject detailing how to love one another as Jesus loves us. (See *"Unlocking the Mystery of Marriage: Loving Your Spouse the Way Christ Loves the Church."*) This is only possible because it is a blessed union that portrays the relationship believers enjoy with our Lord.

God created men and women with differing strengths, weaknesses, and qualities that complement and complete each other. Unlike all of the other beings in creation, God took one of Adam's ribs to create Eve. In marriage, the two once again "become one flesh" to fully reflect God's image. The intimacy between husband and wife is the closest two human beings can ever be to one another, and it foreshadows the spiritual intimacy we will share with our Lord when He returns for us to join Him in the marriage supper of the Lamb:

"Let us rejoice and be glad and give the glory to Him, for the marriage of the Lamb has come and His bride has made herself ready." (Revelation 19:7)

The marriage relationship is also one that gives ample opportunities to put the grace and forgiveness of God on display which are both central to the Gospel message. When two fallen, sinful humans are joined together through the ups and downs of life, there are bound to be times when sins against the other cause hurt or pain. This allows us the opportunity to seek and extend forgiveness and to offer grace and mercy as Christ does for us. God can use this relationship to sanctify us as He makes us more like Jesus.

What quality could be more like Jesus than sacrificial love? Daily, we are asked to lay down our wants and needs for the well-being of another. Learning to put others before ourselves is central to a loving marriage and family, and when we do, we are most like Him.

Fellowship

Although marriage and family are the pillars of society, relationships with friends, especially with fellow believers who are our brothers and sisters in Christ, are extremely important and vital to our health and happiness.

But how does the Bible make sense of our need for this fellowship? To answer that question let's look more closely at our Triune God. Throughout His Word, we have seen Him revealed as three persons in one God—God the Father, God the Son, and God the Holy Spirit.

The Athanasian Creed, a statement of Christian faith dating back as far as the 5th century, explains the Trinity like this:

That we worship one God in Trinity, and Trinity in Unity, neither confounding the Persons, nor dividing the Substance. For there is one Person of the Father, another of the Son, and another of the Holy Ghost. But the Godhead of the Father, of the Son, and of the Holy Ghost, is all one, the Glory equal, the Majesty co-eternal. Such as the Father is, such is the Son, and such is the Holy Ghost.

God has fellowship with Himself within this Trinitarian arrangement. Because He is a relational God and has created us in His image, we were made for relationships both with Him and with others.

The concept of the Trinity is a mystery that is extremely difficult, if not impossible, for our finite minds to comprehend, yet we cannot deny that it is how God has revealed Himself to us in His Word. The Bible gives several examples of the Trinity throughout its pages. Here are some key examples:

After being baptized, Jesus came up immediately from the water; and behold, the heavens were opened, and he saw the Spirit of God descending as a dove and lighting on Him, and behold, a voice out of the heavens said, "This is My beloved Son, in whom I am well-pleased." (Matthew 3:16-17)

Go therefore and make disciples of all the nations, baptizing them in the name of the Father and the Son and the Holy Spirit. (Matthew 28:19)

God the Father, Jesus the Son, and the Holy Spirit have existed as the one true God in three persons from eternity past and will continue to exist eternally in the future. Because they enjoy a perfect relationship, and we are created in His image, we are also created for relationships.

Just to touch a little more on this enormous topic, let's first look at three irrefutable claims from Scripture to help us better understand the concept of the Trinity. The following verses show us how the Trinity exists in three equal persons, yet is still one God.

The Father is God:

Yet for us there is one God, the Father, from whom are all things and for whom we exist, (1 Corinthians 8:6a)

The Son is God:

And one Lord, Jesus Christ, through whom are all things and through whom we exist. (1 Corinthians 8:6b)

"I and the Father are one." (Jesus speaking in John 10:30)

In the beginning was the Word, and the Word was with God, and the Word was God. (John 1:1)

The Gospel of John tells us that Jesus is that Word:

And the Word became flesh, and dwelt among us, and we saw His glory, glory as of the only begotten from the Father, full of grace and truth. (John 1:14)

For in Him all the fullness of Deity dwells in bodily form. (Paul speaking of Jesus in Colossians 2:9)

The Holy Spirit is God:

"When the Helper comes, whom I will send to you from the Father, that is the Spirit of truth who proceeds from the Father, He will testify about Me, (Jesus speaking in John 15:6)

But Peter said, "Ananias, why has Satan filled your heart to lie to the Holy Spirit and to keep back some of the price of the land? While it remained unsold, did it not remain your own? And after it was sold, was it not under your control? Why is it that you have conceived this deed in your heart? You have not lied to men but to God." (Acts 5:3-4)

Yet there is only one God:

"Hear, O Israel! The LORD is our God, the LORD is one!"
(Deuteronomy 6:4)

"Thus says the LORD, the King of Israel and his
Redeemer, the LORD of hosts: 'I am the first and I am
the last, and there is no God besides Me.'" (Isaiah 44:6)

"When the Helper comes, whom I will send to you from
the Father, that is the Spirit of truth who proceeds
from the Father, He will testify about Me," (Jesus
speaking in John 15:26)

The Trinity is too profound for the human mind to comprehend fully, yet it is seen throughout the Bible. (For a more detailed explanation of the doctrine of the Trinity, see the full Athanasian Creed online.)

Our Relationships Reflect God's Glory and Design

We are all God's creation, but we become part of His family when we are born again and adopted as His children through faith in our Lord Jesus. As fellow believers, we become brothers and sisters to one another because we share the same spiritual Father. Maybe you've met someone new and as soon as you found out they were a believer you felt an instant connection with them. Fellow believers and church members can be some of our closest friends because we share the same Father and are indwelled by the Holy

Spirit who unites us in fellowship. As a spiritual family, those relationships can be one of our greatest sources of love and joy. But they can also be the cause of some of our deepest hurts. That is because we also still share a common sin nature that we will continue to battle as long as we are on this side of heaven. None of us goes to church because we are perfect, but rather because we know we are not. No church is perfect because it is filled with sinners desperately in need of a savior.

Just as in marriage and natural families, the effects of the curse of sin still touch all of us and our relationships from time to time. Yet, the perfect will of our God is that we live together in unity. Jesus prayed this for His followers (and for all of us who would follow Him through their testimony), shortly before His crucifixion and resurrection:

That they may all be one; even as You, Father, are in Me and I in You, that they also may be in Us, so that the world may believe that You sent Me. (John 17:21)

That oneness shared by the Holy Trinity is something God desires for us as the family of God. Our fellowship here, as wonderful and yet imperfect as it may be, is a foretaste of the perfect fellowship we will all share in heaven someday.

In each of our earthly relationships, whether family with parents and children, marriage between husbands and wives, or fellowship with friends and other believers, God has ordained these connections to picture various aspects of Himself and our communion with Him. These relationships are just more practical examples of how the Bible makes life make sense.

Chapter 7: Vocations

For this reason also, since the day we heard of it, we have not ceased to pray for you and to ask that you may be filled with the knowledge of His will in all spiritual wisdom and understanding, so that you will walk in a manner worthy of the Lord, to please Him in all respects, bearing fruit in every good work and increasing in the knowledge of God; (Colossians 1:9-10)

Education: Why Do We Learn?

This may sound like an obvious question, or perhaps it's not something you've ever even considered. Learning is just what we do naturally from the time we're born. But, does the Bible give us insight into why we learn, work, and rest? Our opening verse suggests that it does, and it gives us reasons why.

In our modern age, we have access to an abundance of information at our fingertips. If we want to know what year our favorite movie star was born, what makes mosquito bites itch, why flamingos are pink, or why dogs eat grass, a quick internet search gives us the answer in seconds. The time between not knowing something and knowing it has become dramatically shorter than in previous generations. But knowing facts and having true wisdom are completely different concepts. Wisdom is the correct application of knowledge. An Irish rugby player named Brian O'Driscoll once said, "Knowledge is knowing that a tomato is a fruit. Wisdom is knowing not to put it in a fruit salad."[14]

The ability of the human mind to learn new information is astounding. Our Creator has given us complex brains with a huge capacity to process concepts, facts, and ideas because He, too, is a complex, creative, and infinitely intelligent being. He is the source of all wisdom and truth. One of the world's greatest scientists, Johannes Kepler, stated that learning is merely "thinking God's thoughts after Him."[15] Anything we as humans try to discover, God already knows. We are simply trying to figure out how He did what He did.

The world often cries out "Trust the science!" and to some degree, that is true. However, man's understanding of science continually changes as we learn new information and grow in our knowledge of how God designed this world. How many of us avoided

---

[14] Brian O'Driscoll, Brainy Quote, accessed January 26, 2024, https://www.brainyquote.com/authors/brian-odriscoll-quotes.

[15] Kenneth Ham, "Thinking God's Thoughts after Him," Institute for Creation Research, October 1, 1991, https://www.icr.org/article/thinking-gods-thoughts-after-him.

eating eggs or butter for years thinking they were bad for our health, only to discover now that they can be an important part of a balanced diet? When we only trust human discoveries without going to God first, we are simply putting our faith in man's word, and man is notoriously unreliable.

I find it fascinating and highly ironic that so many unbelievers who do not trust the Bible often discredit it by claiming it is "just a book written by men," although we've seen it was actually authored by God and merely penned by men. Yet, every science textbook we have, and even Charles Darwin's book *"On the Origin of Species"* upon which many build their entire worldview, was authored by mere humans. This once again shows us the battle for authority between God and man as highlighted in chapter 5. It's no wonder that the devil's first lie, which led to the fall of man, was a quest for knowledge. By eating from the "Tree of the Knowledge of Good and Evil," man sought to achieve the impossible feat of knowing everything that God knows, rather than just trusting the ultimate source of knowledge Himself. The Bible tells us this would still happen and gives us wise counsel about avoiding this situation:

See to it that no one takes you captive by philosophy and empty deceit, according to human tradition, according to the elemental spirits of the world, and not according to Christ. (Colossians 2:8, ESV)

Trust in the Lord with all your heart and do not lean on your own understanding. In all your ways acknowledge Him, and He will make your paths straight. (Proverbs 3:5-6)

True knowledge and wisdom can only reliably come from God who knows all things and from the solid foundation of the Word in which He has revealed Himself to us. The Bible tells us that when we put God first, that is where true learning and understanding begin:

The fear of the LORD is the beginning of knowledge; Fools despise wisdom and instruction. (Proverbs 1:7)

Even Jesus, who is fully God and fully man, submitted Himself to the limits of our human condition when He came to earth to live among us. The Bible tells us that He subjected Himself to the same learning process that we all experience:

And Jesus kept increasing in wisdom and stature, and in favor with God and men. (Luke 2:52)

Although He was a Son, He learned obedience from the things which He suffered. (Hebrews 5:8)

If the Son of God in human flesh needed to learn, how much more do we? Jesus laid aside His divine privileges to experience all we do as humans and fully relate to us. Because of this, He can empathize with us in our weaknesses. God promises that when we sincerely seek Him and ask for wisdom, He will grant that request:

If any of you lacks wisdom, let him ask God, who gives generously to all without reproach, and it will be given him. (James 1:5, ESV)

Education and learning play a central role in each of our lives to varying degrees. God commands parents to train their children and teach them His ways. We go to school from our early years to learn reading, writing, and arithmetic. Then, we pursue additional education to master trades and careers so we can be productive members of society and help our fellow man. Many universities were started by Christians including Harvard, Yale, and Princeton. Education helps us make sense of the world in which we live while training us to make a living and to make a life for ourselves and our families.

Yet the purpose of learning and education is not merely to attain a job or career, or to make money and acquire possessions, because those temporal goods and achievements will eventually pass away. We learn so that we can best serve and glorify God in all that we do. As we learn new things, we begin to grasp and marvel at the vastness of His wisdom, and we stand in awe of His power and magnificence. Ultimately, we learn so that we can know Him better and love Him more!

Much of God's creation has the capacity to learn, including animals that can be trained, but only people can imagine, reason, and create because we have been made in the image of our infinitely creative God. Only humans can create beautiful pieces of music and art and fully appreciate beauty and design. We are also the only part of His creation that can verbally communicate thoughts, ideas, and feelings in elaborate and complex ways. God created language, which in itself is a fascinating and sophisticated topic. Have you ever considered just how language came to be or how when we say a word like "red," another person knows exactly what we mean? How do the letters, r-e-d even communicate a concept like color? It's mind-boggling, yet God made us so intricately and amazingly that we could learn and process such complexities.

We are thinking beings because our God is the infinite "thinker." When I was quite young, I remember imagining that if I spent time each day learning everything I could about every different subject in the world, I would eventually know all that was possible to know. As a naïve child, I had no idea of the infinite knowledge of God. We spend our entire lifetimes learning how the world works when we are merely discovering how God accomplished everything He did! Ken Ham of Answers in Genesis states it this way:

"The Bible doesn't merely answer what science cannot— the Bible provides the very foundation and framework for science. It's only because there is an eternal, consistent, orderly God who created the earth and universe that we can study creation, trusting that the laws of nature (which are immaterial) will apply the same in the future as they did yesterday and still do today. If the universe is the result of a random, chance process, we can't know this! It's only because the Bible is true and the Creator God exists that we have a foundation for science."[16]

From exploring the complexities of our DNA in biology to studying the speed of light in physics, calculating elaborate concepts in calculus, or defining difficult words in language studies, our quest for knowledge is a never-ending process. No matter how old we are or how long we live, we will only scratch the surface of attaining the vast expanse of available truth and learning that is possible. But when we have a Biblical worldview as our starting point, we build on a solid foundation of truth. Our Lord Jesus *is* that truth (see John 14:6).

True knowledge begins with reverence and humility before our creator and redeemer. That is why God and His Word need to be foundational to all we know and learn and to each aspect of our lives. It's only through the Bible that life truly makes any sense!

That their hearts may be encouraged, having been knit together in love, and attaining to all the wealth that comes from the full assurance of understanding, resulting in a true knowledge of God's mystery, that is,

---

[16] Ken Ham, "Science Can't Explain Everything," Answers in Genesis, November 29, 2023, https://answersingenesis.org/blogs/ken-ham/2023/11/29/science-cant-explain-everything/.

Christ Himself, in whom are hidden all the treasures of wisdom and knowledge. (Colossians 2:2-3)

Work

Just as God created us with the ability and opportunity to learn and grow, our vocations help us to live purposeful and fulfilling lives and to glorify Him in whatever occupations He calls us to do. We work because our God is a working God. The Bible tells us that He created the world in six days and on the seventh day He rested from His labors:

For in six days the LORD made the heavens and the earth, the sea and all that is in them, and rested on the seventh day; therefore the LORD blessed the sabbath day and made it holy. (Exodus 20:11)

Although since the fall of man, work often feels like drudgery or at times even punishment, this was not God's original plan. Even in the perfection of the Garden of Eden, He created Adam and instructed him to work the land before he and Eve fell into sin:

The LORD God took the man and put him in the garden of Eden to work it and keep it. (Genesis 2:15, ESV)

It was only after sin entered the world that our labor became toilsome:

Then to Adam He said, "Because you have listened to the voice of your wife, and have eaten from the tree about which I commanded you, saying, 'You shall not eat from it' Cursed is the ground because of you; In toil you will eat of it all the days of your life." (Genesis 3:17)

Although work can be difficult and exhausting at times, it can also be a source of enjoyment, fulfillment, and accomplishment. The average employed person spends about 70,000 hours of their life at their job.[17] God gifts each of us with different talents, abilities, desires, and opportunities to serve Him through the vocations to which He calls us. Whether a young mom raising children at home, a laborer making products that make our life easier, an engineer using God-given creativity to design new ways to improve systems and processes, or a healthcare worker helping to keep us healthy, our work is a way to give us purpose and meaning. Work and the ability to do it are gifts from Him, even when it doesn't feel like it!

Although work can fulfill us with meaning and satisfaction, just like everything else in life, it ultimately allows us the opportunity to glorify God. The Bible tells us that when we do our work, we should do it for Him. When we do it with excellence and to the best of our ability, it gives Him glory as others see us and we represent Him well:

---

[17] Sarah Long, "30 Bible Verses About Work," PushPay, September 8, 2023, https://pushpay.com/blog/30-bible-verses-about-work/.

"Let your light shine in front of men. Then they will see the good things you do and will honor your Father who is in heaven." (Matthew 5:16)

Whatever you do, do your work heartily, as for the Lord rather than for men, knowing that from the Lord you will receive the reward of the inheritance. It is the Lord Christ whom you serve. (Colossians 3:23-24)

Through our labors, God enables us to provide for ourselves and others. To some, He gives less, and to others more, but through it all, we are given the opportunity to grow closer to Him and be made more like Jesus as we steward our belongings wisely.

God also gives us ample opportunity to trust Him and turn to Him in every aspect of our lives, including those related to our work. When we search for employment, we can seek Him in prayer to ask Him to guide us and provide what we need. When tasks are difficult, or situations arise that trouble us, we can pray and ask Him to help and comfort us. When work is going well, or even when it isn't, we can thank and praise Him rejoicing in His blessings and in the satisfaction it brings. From the good gifts He provides through our employment, we have the opportunity to be generous and help others in need.

Wherever God leads us to work also provides us with a mission field. Each person He brings into our lives, whether a customer or a co-worker, is another soul God wants to reach with the Gospel of our Lord Jesus Christ.

As we go into our workplaces each week, we are allowed access to reach people that even full-time ministers never could—people who would never set foot into a church or hear them preach. This shows us that all believers are missionaries, sent into the field to glorify God and reach others for Christ. Even a stay-at-home mom has her own mission field of young people entrusted to her care whom she can reach for Jesus. This gives our vocations even more purpose and meaning than just accomplishing the job itself. It gives us a reason to get up in the morning with a fresh start and new opportunities to serve the Lord.

By giving us purpose, fulfillment, provisions, and opportunities to trust, glorify, and serve God, our vocations are a blessing and a gift from Him, once again showing us that the Bible gives meaning to work and makes it make sense!

Rest

With work comes a need for rest. For practical reasons, we can see why it is necessary. But, have you ever considered why it is Biblical? We rest because God rested. When He created the world in six days, He dedicated the seventh day as a Sabbath from His labors. Of course, God did not need to rest physically like we do, as His power and strength are limitless. However, because He instituted a day of rest, it shows us that the concept itself has significant practical and spiritual meaning. Practically, it was designed as a rest from our labors, and spiritually, it was a sign of the covenant between God and His people as they set aside one day each week to be wholly devoted to Him:

"Remember the Sabbath day, to keep it holy. Six days you shall labor, and do all your work, but the seventh day is a Sabbath to the Lord your God. On it you shall not do any work," (Exodus 20:8-10a)

If we are working for 70,000+ hours of our lives, it is obvious that we need regular physical rest. Each night, the Lord gives us the gift of sleep so we can recharge our strength and so that our bodies can repair themselves from the day's work. Sleep restores our physical, mental, and emotional health in a way nothing else can. It promotes immune function, heart health, weight control, improved mood and memory, and reduces stress and inflammation. Lack of sleep is detrimental to all aspects of our lives including relationships, work, health, behavior, attitude, and learning, and it increases our risk for infections, accidents, obesity, depression, and other chronic health problems.[18]

Another benefit of nightly sleep is that it gives us a new beginning each day with a chance to start fresh, and it reminds us of the transformed life we have in Christ when we come to Him in faith. The Bible tells us His mercies are *"new every morning"* (see Lamentations

---

[18] "What Are Sleep Deprivation and Deficiency?" National Heart, Lung, and Blood Institute, accessed January 27, 2024, https://www.nhlbi.nih.gov/health/sleep-deprivation.

3:22-23). In the Old Testament, the Lord instituted various Sabbath rests for His people and even for the land, which we now know is important so the soil can replenish vital nutrients to support the growth of crops. This gave both the people and the land a fresh start to be productive in their work.

But rest isn't always just about sleep or bodily renewal. Jesus refreshes our spirits throughout the day when we come to Him in prayer and His Word. He comforts us and gives us relief from our worries and cares. Our hearts and minds can know true rest when we turn our eyes on Him and away from our circumstances. This is where we find peace amid troubles and trials that only He can give:

You keep him in perfect peace whose mind is stayed on You, because he trusts in You. (Isaiah 26:3, ESV)

In an even more important way, when we come to Jesus by grace through faith, He gives us rest from "working our way to heaven." By completing the work of our salvation on the cross, He took the burden from us and carried it Himself. When Jesus said, "It is finished," before He died, He provided us with the rest of knowing we no longer have to strive to please God or earn our heavenly reward. All other religions involve "work" on our part to be saved, yet through Jesus, we have rest in knowing we are at peace with God through Him:

"Come to Me, all who are weary and heavy-laden, and I will give you rest. Take My yoke upon you and learn

from Me, for I am gentle and humble in heart, and YOU
WILL FIND REST FOR YOUR SOULS. *For My yoke is easy
and My burden is light." (Matthew 11:28-30)*

Jesus is saying we can stop working to try to earn our
way to heaven because He's already done the work for
us. Because of Him, we can know we are secure forever.
This brings us to the ultimate picture of rest: eternity in
heaven with Him. The Sabbath that God designed from
the beginning of creation pointed to this reality. Not
only can we rest physically, emotionally, and mentally
here on earth, but we will rest spiritually for all eternity
with Him through the finished work of our Lord Jesus
Christ. The Bible paints this beautiful picture for us:

*So there remains a Sabbath rest for the people of God.
For the one who has entered His rest has himself also
rested from his works, as God did from His. (Hebrews
4:9-10)*

If we are in Christ, one day we will rest from our labors
here and enter an eternal peace with Him in heaven.
That is how the Bible makes rest make sense!

Chapter 8: Society

He has made everything appropriate in its time. He has also set eternity in their heart, yet so that man will not find out the work which God has done from the beginning even to the end. (Ecclesiastes 3:11)

People want to be spiritual, but they don't want to be accountable. This thought occurred to me several times over the years as I have seen many people seeking meaning and purpose in all forms of religion worldwide. Spirituality is a broad concept covering all types of mystical or religious experiences. It usually involves some connection with a belief in the supernatural, a divine being, or a higher power. From the beginning of time, human beings have sought these spiritual experiences. Generally, they have cultural implications or influences, and often people create a god that agrees with their convictions, preferences, or understanding of the world as they perceive it.

But the reason man has always sought religion or spirituality is that God has put eternity in our hearts (see Ecclesiastes 3:11). He has sought a personal relationship with us since He created the first man and woman, Adam and Eve, and has chosen to communicate with us through His Word. We don't need to imagine a god of our own making or seek understanding from ever-changing, fleeting sources because God has revealed Himself to us in the flesh and blood person of Jesus Christ who came to this earth to dwell among us and save us.

We can know the one, true, eternal God through the revelation He has given us through the Bible. Through its pages, we can learn who He is and what He is like. As we've seen, God's Word also gives us purpose, meaning, direction, guidance, and reasons why the world is the way it is. We can submit to God as He has revealed Himself or deny His authority (for now), but ultimately, God's Word and His ways make sense out of every aspect of life. People want a sense of spirituality but do not want to be accountable to God's authority over their lives. If they admit that He exists and has standards for us, they must acknowledge that they are accountable to Him. The concept of submission has often had a negative connotation to mankind who is naturally rebellious in this sinful, fallen state. But submission among people does not mean inferiority. It is simply God's order and way of protecting and providing for us.

Order and Authority

Let every person be subject to the governing authorities. For there is no authority except from God, and those that exist have been instituted by God. (Romans 13:1, ESV)

One of the most important ways the Bible makes sense of our world is through the concept of authority. We have seen how sin entered the world when the devil rebelled against God's authority and proceeded to get man to follow him in that rebellion. But, God-ordained governance is a beneficial thing, something designed for our well-being and prosperity. Like loving parents who exercise wisdom and influence over their children, God does the same for us. One of the ways He does so is through the ordering and structuring of societal jurisdiction that exists for our protection and provision. An orderly society with benevolent leaders is one of God's gifts to us. Without it, we would have chaos and rampant lawlessness. We live in a structured and orderly world because He is a God of order.

While man tends to balk at the concept of submission, we must acknowledge that it can be beneficial when properly instituted. Take these examples: a police officer has authority over a citizen who is transgressing the law, a pastor has spiritual authority over his congregants as he leads and guides them, a teacher has authority over her students, a parent has authority over his or her child(ren), and a boss has authority over their employees. The ultimate example is that Jesus submitted to His Father's will to die on the cross to save us from our sins as we see here:

Saying, "Father, if You are willing, remove this cup from Me; yet not My will, but Yours be done." (Luke 22:42)

The Holy Spirit teaches and speaks as God directs:

"But when He, the Spirit of truth, comes, He will guide you into all the truth; for He will not speak on His own initiative, but whatever He hears, He will speak; and He will disclose to you what is to come." (John 16:13)

No one would rightly say that Jesus or the Holy Spirit is inferior to the Father, and no one would imply that citizens are less important than police officers, students than teachers, or congregants than their pastor.

Order and submission exist in society for our good. Society functions best when each person is acting according to their God-ordained roles. We need civil government and laws to protect ourselves and each other in this fallen world because man is prone to sin and rebel against God's authority and those that He has established.

Without this orderly design, our world would be in chaos. The book of Judges in the Old Testament has an ominous ending showing us what life is like without God's structure, and which we should heed as a warning to us even today:

In those days there was no king in Israel; everyone did what was right in his own eyes. (Judges 21:25)

It was a time of great apostasy and lawlessness. Without order and authority, we are at the mercy of the consequences of the evil committed by others. We can see even now, a push to rebel against these God-ordained authorities in examples such as "Defund the police" and fighting against our country's constitution as laws that have existed from the beginning are overturned as "unconstitutional." But as long as sin is in the world, we need these systems God has set in place for our benefit. By His mercy and grace, He has instituted civil government and laws for our good. Yes, authority can and has been abused over time, but when God's authority is honored by those in power, they lead and protect in the ways that He designed them to do. Through these institutions, we experience justice and uphold what is morally right and good. Thankfully, God has written this on our hearts as we will see next.

Justice and Morality

For when Gentiles who do not have the Law do instinctively the things of the Law, these, not having the Law, are a law to themselves, in that they show the work of the Law written in their hearts, their conscience bearing witness and their thoughts alternately accusing or else defending them, (Romans 2:14-15)

The Bible is not primarily a rule-book for us to follow although it does have numerous principles and concepts that, when observed, lead to more peaceful living for all of us. But God's law is not a standard we can keep perfectly. The law was established to show us we are sinners who need a Savior because we have broken that law. We don't need to ask ourselves, "What would Jesus do?" as if He were just an example for us to follow—although He definitely is! The real question is "What *did* Jesus do?", which points us to the Gospel and the fact that He fulfilled the law perfectly on our behalf.

Although we cannot keep all of God's standards and must rely on the one who did for us, the Bible also tells us that God has written His law on our hearts. This is why we all share a common morality, given to us by Him. It was out of His love and mercy that He gave us this moral foundation, or the world would be a lot worse than it already is. A clip from the famous 1950-60s TV show, "Leave it to Beaver" summed it up well:

Beaver stated: "You know, Dad, I might be a lot worse kid than I am if I wasn't afraid of being caught doing stuff."

His dad, Ward, replied: "You know, Beaver, I suppose that's true of most all of us."

Our consciences let us know when we have betrayed them. We know when we are guilty of failing to do good or committing wrong. None of us need to be told that murder, rape, lying, and theft are wrong because an internal sense of morality is hard-wired into each of us. We call those things "immoral", yet if God hadn't written His law on our hearts and set a standard for right and wrong, how would we know something is truly immoral? Otherwise, everything would only be a matter of personal preference. His common code of ethics exercised through our consciences is one of the ways He keeps us safe in a world tainted by sin.

Because we inherently know good from evil, we also have a sense of internal justice. There is something inside each of us that cries out for wrongdoing to be punished and virtue to be rewarded. Those who protest that "God lets bad things happen" want to see evil restrained and justice served. Yet how can we even call something "bad" or "good" without a plumbline of truth and righteousness (or "right-ness")? How can we demand justice without a supreme judge?

If we are simply cosmic accidents, who came into being by random chance over time, our complaints are just arbitrary rules decided upon by our fallible, ever-changing source of human wisdom and preference.

Bruce Shelly writes in his book _Christian Theology in Plain Language_, "My argument against God was that the universe seemed so cruel and unjust. But how had I got this idea of just and unjust? A man does not call a line crooked unless he has some idea of a straight line... Thus, in the very act of trying to prove that God did not exist—in other words, that the whole of reality was senseless—I found I was forced to assume that one part of reality—namely my idea of justice—was full of sense."

It's been said that there are two main ways to reach a person. We can either appeal to their intellect and reasoning or their conscience and morality. Although we share a common sense of right and wrong, our natural minds oppose God and cannot receive His truth unless He transforms us through His Word and Spirit.

This means we can't reason someone into believing the Gospel of our Lord Jesus Christ because their hearts and minds are set on living by their own rules and standards rather than God's. Instead, we need to arouse the conscience through the piercing of God's Word, which is called *"the sword of the Spirit"* in Ephesians 6:17. It is when the Spirit acts through the use of Scripture to convict a person of sin and righteousness that they can call out to God for forgiveness and salvation.

I once debated a man whose stated purpose was to "de-weaponize the Bible" and promote tolerance and inclusivity of all manner of things that God opposes. But, God Himself called His Word a weapon when He said it was sharper than any two-edged sword and could pierce and divide both soul and spirit and discern the thoughts and intents of our hearts (see Hebrews 4:12).

Some think God should just be loving without meting out justice. But that is unloving to the victims of crime. To let a criminal go free without retribution is a horrible injustice to those he has harmed or victimized. It's because God loves us so much that He despises and punishes sin just as a parent detests anything evil that might come against his or her child. How can we be indignant against injustice, yet consider God unloving if He upholds it? Every sin ever committed by every person will receive punishment—either by the sinner himself or by Jesus who took our sins to the cross.

It is only because people *"suppress the truth in unrighteousness,"* that sin and evil continue to permeate our world today:

For the wrath of God is revealed from heaven against all ungodliness and unrighteousness of men who suppress the truth in unrighteousness, because that which is known about God is evident within them; for God made it evident to them. For since the creation of the world His invisible attributes, His eternal power and divine nature, have been clearly seen, being understood through what has been made, so that they are without excuse. For even though they knew God, they did not honor Him as God or give thanks, but they became futile in their speculations, and their foolish heart was darkened. Professing to be wise, they became fools. (Romans 1:18-22)

This is so prevalent in our current age. Truth is now considered relative, and absolute truth is denied and suppressed so that people can live according to their sinful desires. God has made Himself known through creation, His Word, and the person and work of Jesus Christ. Yet man continues to rebel. Professing to be wise, they have become fools in the eyes of our all-seeing, all-knowing God, the source of all truth and righteousness.

Because the Bible is a living and active book, God's power working through it can fully transform hearts and minds and bring people to a saving knowledge of the truth. This brings us full circle back to the beginning of this book, as we've seen how God's book makes all areas of life make sense. The Bible is so amazing and powerful because it points us to God and has everything we need to help us make sense of this world and look forward to the next!

Conclusion

A member of the Gideons International organization once spoke at a church on a Sunday morning, relating a story of one of their members who was preaching the Gospel on a college campus. As the man spoke, a student held up a copy of the New Testament which a Gideon's member had just handed to him. The student screamed aloud that he was a Satanist and that he only followed Satan. He then attempted to take his lighter to the Scriptures in his hand. As he fumbled with it the lighter failed to burn God's sacred words. Frustrated, angry, and somewhat surprised, the student left hastily. However, shortly after that incident, he returned to the scene and humbly asked the preaching man what power this book must hold to cause this incredible occurrence. It was then that the student heard and believed the Gospel, and prayed to receive Jesus Christ as his Savior and Lord. Not only that but three other students watching this transformation and hearing the Gospel themselves also prayed to receive Christ that day. Only the Spirit of God working through the power of His Word can accomplish such a dramatic conversion in a person's life.

Not only is the Bible living, active, and powerful, it also explains how and why the world works the way it does. No other worldview has all the answers the way a Biblical worldview does:

It answers all of life's big questions, like why are we here? How did we get here? How do we live while we are here? Where are we going, and how do we get there? Why is there evil in the world, and what's the solution to it?

- It tells us why we have relationships like families, marriages, and friendships—and how to best navigate them.
- It explains why we learn, work, and rest.
- It shows us how life is structured through order and authority for our well-being and prosperity.
- It explains why we have an internal sense of morality and justice.
- It covers the entire span of human behavior and the full spectrum of human emotion.
- Its principles and truths are timeless and apply to us as much today as they did to their original audience.

Most importantly, the Bible is one cohesive storyline of God's plan to save us through our Lord Jesus Christ.

This beautiful text found in the introduction of every Bible produced by Gideons International explains it perfectly:

"The Bible contains the mind of God, the state of man, the way of salvation, the doom of sinners, and the happiness of believers.

Its doctrines are holy, its precepts are binding, its histories are true, and its decisions are immutable.

Read it to be wise, believe it to be safe, and practice it to be holy.

It contains light to direct you, food to support you, and comfort to cheer you.

It is the traveler's map, the pilgrim's staff, the pilot's compass, the soldier's sword, and the Christian's charter.

Here too, Heaven is opened and the gates of Hell disclosed.

Christ is its grand subject, our good its design, and the glory of God its end.

It should fill the memory, rule the heart, and guide the feet.

Read it slowly, frequently, and prayerfully.

It is a mine of wealth, a paradise of glory, and a river of pleasure.

It is given you in life, will be opened at the judgment, and be remembered forever.

It involves the highest responsibility, rewards the greatest labor, and will condemn all who trifle with its sacred contents."[19]

In Summary...

The Bible is living and active and is the only book ever written by a divine Author with the power to transform hearts, minds, and lives. It answers all of life's big questions, and is the one book that truly gives us purpose and makes life make sense—not only for this world but for all of eternity!

---

[19] Justin Taylor, "What Is This Book?" The Gospel Coalition, October 15, 2018, https://www.thegospelcoalition.org/blogs/justin-taylor/what-is-this-book/.

About the Author

Heather Erdmann is a Christian wife, mom, dental hygienist, devotional writer for Lifeway, and best-selling author. She loves helping Christian women grow in their knowledge of the Bible and pointing them to Jesus. Her experience includes online training from Southeastern Baptist Theological Seminary and the Biblical Counseling Institute. For over 30 years she has written devotions and Bible studies for women, taught children's Sunday School and Vacation Bible school, and participated in homeschool curriculum development. She also plays flute and oboe for her local church worship team. When not working or writing, she loves drinking coffee with friends, studying the Bible, cuddling (or napping with) her kitties, taking day trips with her family, or camping with her husband.

You can read more at www.thebiblebasedlife.com and see her available books there or on Amazon.

Other Books by Heather Erdmann

Unlocking the Mystery of Marriage: Loving Your Spouse the Way Christ Loves the Church

A Week in the Word: 12-Week Bible Study Journal

FREE Bible Study Tools Videos

Have you wanted to study the Bible for yourself but have no idea where to start?

Do you want to go deeper into God's Word but aren't sure how?

If you've ever felt unsure of yourself in group Bible studies or even in your own quiet time with the Lord—this is for you!

Scan this QR code to join the FREE "5-Day Bible Study Tools VIDEO Challenge" and learn how to study the Bible for yourself in just 5 days!

Note from the Author:

If you have enjoyed this book or found it helpful in any way, would you please share a review on Amazon.com to help spread the message of the Gospel and the importance of building our lives on the solid foundation of God's Word? Thank you!

www.ingramcontent.com/pod-product-compliance
Lightning Source LLC
Chambersburg PA
CBHW071334150726
47997CB00002B/722